ST ALBION
PARISH NEWS

BOOK 8

Published in Great Britain by
Private Eye Productions Ltd, 6 Carlisle Street, W1D 3BN.
© 2005 Pressdram Ltd
ISBN 1 901784 35 5
Designed by Bridget Tisdall
Printed and bound by
Butler and Tanner Ltd, Frome and London
2 4 6 8 10 9 7 5 3 1

VICAR ON THE SPOT!

ST ALBION PARISH NEWS
BOOK 8

Further letters from the vicar,
the Rev. A.R.P. Blair MA (Oxon)

compiled for

PRIVATE EYE

by Ian Hislop, Richard Ingrams,
Christopher Booker and Barry Fantoni

*Some of our more Catholic readers
may find this beautiful icon of
"Our Lady of the Mantilla" helpful
in focusing on their devotions.*

*Reciting a couple of "Hail Cheries!"
will add to the intensity of the
spiritual experience.*

Father Tony Blair

ST ALBION PARISH NEWS

1st October 2004

Hullo!

And the first thing I want to make clear to you all – as I will be stressing on this week's parish outing to Brighton – is that I'm back!

Not that I have ever been away! No, but some people might have thought I was away, especially when they saw all those pictures of me being away on holiday that Mr Prescott put in this newsletter while I was away!

Anyway, I was never away in any real sense. As it says in the Holy Scripture, "Hey, I am with you always" (*Book of Job For Life*, Chapter 5).

But enough of that. What I want to talk about today – and I want you to talk about it too! – is this week's Good News!

The First Great Crusade is over! Whether you were in favour of it or not, all that is now in the past!

Whatever you thought at the time, whether you were for us or against us, a hawk or a dove – it's over! Done! Finito!, as my friend Monsignor Berlusconi might put it (and, incidentally, memo to Mr Prescott, it was not a *banana* on Silvio's head, it was a *bandana*, which is quite a different thing, as those of us who were fortunate enough to have a proper education know only too well. No offence, John, you fat oik!).

(DO YOU REALLY WANT THIS BIT TO GO IN, TONY? D. Hill. Ed.)

Anyway, as I was saying, let's put the First Crusade behind us!

It really is time to move on, which is why we are now poised to launch our Second Great Crusade, which will be even more glorious and successful than the First Crusade, under the inspired leadership of the same team, including our good friends the Rev. Dubya, Brother Rumsfeld and Sister Condy.

And this time all decent, reasonable, sensible people, I am sure, will be right behind us! Because this time there can be no doubt that we are confronted by pure evil, "awesome in its evilitude", as the Rev. Dubya so memorably put it in his "Mission Accomplished" statement.

Perhaps now that we are all united, we can put this whole question of the war behind us, and start to think about the things which really matter, nearer to home!

Just consider some of the really exciting new initiatives which we are launching this autumn, to mark the beginning of the Church's year!

- *Mrs Hewitt's new plan for women to have more babies, and then go out to work.*

Patricia will be giving a talk on this important issue at this week's parish outing, including helpful hints on how to make babies with your partner (of either sex, of course!).

- *Up With The Fox, Down With The Cruel Foxhunters!*

Not that I personally have anything against the people who want to hunt with dogs, like our good friend Mrs Mallalieu, which is why I was very careful not to be present at the PCC meeting when this came up for yet another discussion. I honestly think we have talked about this long enough, and it's time to move on and draw a line under it once and for all. So the hunt will definitely not be meeting outside the vicarage after 2012, unless Mr Michael can come up with some rather more helpful compromise in the next few days! Not, of course, that I want in any way to compromise on what I know many of you regard as a core belief in your faith. But for that very reason, I think we'd better just wait and see what happens, shall we?

Obviously, there are plenty of other important topics for us all to talk about this week in Brighton, but I don't want to spoil it all by letting on what they are!

So I hope we're all going to enjoy our week by the seaside, and that no one is going to try to hog the limelight by making a silly, self-serving speech, as happened last year. I don't want to name names, but all of you who were there will remember the man who stood up and tried to pretend that he could do my job better than I can, instead of getting on with the one job he is really fitted for, ie counting up the 2p pieces in the church collection (and probably getting that wrong as well! No offence, Gordon, just my little joke!).

Yours, Tony

Congratulations!

The Vicar's wife has been chosen to give an after-lunch speech to some very important American Pet Insurance agents as a replacement for Lauren Bacall!

What an amazing tribute to Cherie, as a successful woman in her own right, that she is now considered to be in the same league as a Hollywood superstar! She will be talking on the subject "What it's like being married to the Vicar".

St Albion's Ramblers

Mr Michael regrets that he will be unable to join the "Right To Roam" ramble next Tuesday,

due to an unprecedented pressure of work. He has had to cancel all his commitments for the foreseeable future, and will spend his time locked in his basement with a six-months' supply of Kendal Mint Cake and bottled water. Parishioners are reminded that the "right to roam" stops at Mr Michael's front door, and the local riot police are already on standby to beat over the head any members of the St Albion's Countryside Alliance who are rash enough to come within 100 metres of Mr Michael's home. You have been warned.

A.M. (PCC Representative for Rambling and Country Issues)

The Leader of the United Reformed Democratic Liberal Church steps up his campaign to take over the parish. By Mr de la Nougerede

Brighton Rock!!!

Undoubtedly the highspot of this week's parish outing will be the chance to see, hear and even meet, the amazing Mr Bono, the now legendary "rocker"-turned-evangelist on behalf of the world's underprivileged. Older parishioners will, of course, remember Mr de Bono ("Ed", as some of us know him), who was so famous in the 1980s with his band "Lateral Thinking". I am so excited by the thought of having a real star in our midst that I am thinking of getting out my trusty old Stratocaster and having a "jam session" with Mr de Bonio! Rock on!

Parish Postbag

From Lady Melvina Barg

Dear Sir,

I would like to apologise to the Vicar and his good lady for the totally unforgiveable behaviour of my husband Melvyn for suggesting that Tony was thinking of resigning for family reasons. I don't know what got into Melvyn, or rather I do – a huge quantity of drink! It would be much better for everybody if my husband stuck to what he is good at, ie drinking (Surely "making arts programmes"? D.H.), and left the writing of books with the Vicar's wife to me.

Incidentally, I shall be doing a "signing" with Ms Booth (ie, the Vicar's wife!) in the St Albion's Bookshop, which is behind Dirty Des's Adult Books And Mags Emporium on the High Street, between Tesco and Tesco.

Cherie tells me that attendance is not "compulsory", but she assures me that anyone who does not buy a copy cannot expect to remain in the Vicar's good books for much longer!

Lady Melvina Barg,
Southbank Road.

(The Editor reserves the right to print all letters defending the Vicar in full. D.H.)

From Fiona Millar

Dear Sir,

I was most interested to read the Vicar's wife's new book (written for her by someone else, incidentally!). In the days when I was working for her, she was perfectly sane and sensible. But then she let in that witch Carol and since then

Yours faithfully,
Fiona Millar (aka Mrs Alastair Campbell, the former editor of the newsletter),
The Old Dossier House, Hutton Road.

(The Editor reserves the right to cut all letters from disloyal former employees of the Vicar for reasons of space. D.H.)

From Sir Rorold of Bremner

Dear Sir,

I used to be a great admirer of the Vicar when he was very popular, but recently I have noticed that everyone hates him, so it is therefore with deep regret that I shall not be playing tennis with him after the service on a Sunday ever again unless he comes to his senses and becomes very popular again

Yours insincerely,
Sir Rorold of Bremner,
Enfield Road, Luvvies Close.

(The Editor reserves the right to cut all letters from disloyal former friends of the Vicar for reasons of space. D.H.)

ST ALBION PARISH NEWS

15th October 2004

Somewhere in Africa

Hullo!

And I don't mind telling you, the last few weeks have been pretty mad!

There was all the excitement of the parish outing to Brighton – which, though I say it myself, was a huge success! And I'd particularly like to thank our new curate, Mr Milburn, for describing my closing address as "probably the most inspiring sermon ever given by a vicar"!

Thanks, Alan, and may I return the compliment by saying that your own "few words" were pretty impressive! Certainly a lot better than the blustering sweaty ranting of some of the other speakers who misjudged the occasion rather badly (Not for the first time, eh Gordon!) .

Then, after that, I had to take five minutes off work to have a spot of open heart surgery! You'd think there was something wrong with me!

But just for the doubters, let me make it crystal clear that I am now fitter than ever! As Mr Milburn so wittily put it, "Tony, we can see that your heart is really in the job!".

The hospital bed from which the vicar rose so speedily has became an object of veneration and pilgrimage! By local artist Mr de la Nougerede

If anyone is unfit around this parish, I suggest that we look at a certain overweight, pasty-faced, over-excitable treasurer who should perhaps 'get a life'– rather than, as Mr Milburn so humorously put it, trying to 'get your job'!

What a pleasure it is to have our new curate around, always ready with a Geordie joke or a comforting word! What a difference he's already made in the parish! If I was thinking of retiring, which I'm not, by the way, or certainly not for a very long time, then I can't think of anyone better to fill my shoes than young Alan!

Hey, of course I know it's not my decision, and I don't want to be accused of "doing deals" here, but let's face it, say the choice was between Alan and, how can I put it, a less suitable Scottish candidate, then you would hardly need me to tell you which way to vote, would you?

And talking of me not retiring, you may have heard on the parish grapevine that Cherie and I have bought a little 17-bedroom retirement home for when the day comes that Alan and his family move into the vicarage and Cherie and I and little Leo will have to bid you fond farewell!

Obviously that's a very long way ahead, so in the meantime, we're going to do our bit for the housing crisis and become "Good Samaritans", by letting out our new house to needy millionaires, possibly from America or the Middle East!

And then to cap it all, I had the great privilege of leading our mission to Africa, accompanied by that saint of our time, Father Geldolf of the Blessed Order of the Boomtown Rats.

What a truly inspiring experience it was for our African hosts, to be able to listen to the incomparably wise words of Father Bob, as he explained to them in his down-to-earth way how it was time for them to get their "fockin' act together".

If I have one abiding impression of the two days we spent travelling around the various countries we're planning to sort out, it is of how humble it made me feel to be in that vast continent, and to know that perhaps you are the only person who is in a position to help them.

And it also made me realise how small and how trivial are all the things that people campaign about in St Albion's.

Were there ever any "weapons of destruction"? Oh, puh – leease!!! That was never an issue!

The important thing is that Saddam *wanted* to have weapons of mass destruction. And as we know from scripture, the intention is just as sinful as the act!

"A man who looketh upon weapons of mass destruction in his heart deserves to be smitten with fire and brimstone" *(The Moron Bible, revised and updated by the Rev. Dubya, with the assistance of Brother Rumsfeld and Sister Condy)*.

So I'd like to end with an apology. I'm sorry, but I haven't got anything to apologise for!

I may have been misled by other people, who told me all sorts of things that turned out not to be entirely true.

And I'm genuinely sorry for those people, because misleading the vicar is just about the most serious offence I can think of!

But am I sorry for playing such a leading role in the great crusade against the Evil One?

"Am I fock", as Father Bob might put it, in his colourful Gaelic patois!

> Yours for the foreseeable future
> (and even beyond!),
>
> Tony

LIVING SAINT VISITS AFRICA!!

He's the one on the left! A.M.

Thought For The Day

"Do not store up your treasure on earth"

*T*ime and again the Good Book reminds us that we should not worry about our pensions but trust in the Lord to provide (or not, as the case maybe). This should reassure us all, especially those parishioners who may be concerned that they are going to have to work for ever or starve.

And there are some other words of comfort, as rendered in the new Gordeon's Bible that you will find in all good hotel bedrooms!

"Consider the lilies of the field. They toil hard but do not get a pension at the end of it."

And here is another quotation to cheer you up as you face the prospect of a cold winter with nothing to eat:

"It is very hard for a rich man to get into heaven. So you're better off without a pension" *(Mark, 7.3)*. Just think about it!

TB

 Parish Postbag

Dear Sir,

I am delighted to see that the recent report on Iraq has confirmed that I was right all along in every respect.

I hope now that the vicar will finally have the decency to admit that he was utterly and completely

Yours sincerely,

Robin Cook,

Galloway Road.

(The Editor reserves the right to cut all letters from disgraced former members of the PCC on the grounds that such people should be careful about throwing stones when we know what they got up to in the organ loft!)

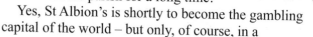

Hullo!

And I'll bet you don't know what I'll be talking about this week! God's gift of Gambling! Feeling lucky? Of course you are, because you've heard the best news to hit the parish for a long time!

Yes, St Albion's is shortly to become the gambling capital of the world – but only, of course, in a responsible way!

There have been a lot of scare stories about how we are going to turn the church into Las Vegas, with rows of slot machines down the nave, and blackjack being played on our communion table!

Honestly! What sort of vicar do you think I am?

Of course there will be slot machines. But only in the vestry, where they can be accessed by responsible parishioners between the hours of nine in the morning and nine the next morning.

As for the blackjack and 'craps' table, this will be out of the way in the crypt, so no worries there!

And, furthermore, Mrs Jowell has personally vetted the highly-respectable and long-established firm from Nevada, Corleone and Capone, which will be installing and running the very limited gaming facilities which will be available on the church premises.

But I know that, despite all our wise and careful precautions, there will still be a small minority of parishioners who will insist that gambling is "sinful"!

What an old-fashioned word and what an old-fashioned attitude!

Nowadays, we read the Bible very differently! And when it says "Thou shalt not encourage thy neighbour to lose everything that he hath, in the vain hope of securing the pot that is jack", we don't now think for a minute that this is suggesting that gambling in itself is in any way a bad thing!

No, what it's saying is that 'responsible' gambling is great! It is as much part of our cultural fabric as the bowling green, the church tower or Mr Desmond's Adult Mags And Videos Centre behind the chip shop and opposite the Binge and Vomit (formerly the Queen's Arms).

And gaming, let's face it, performs a very valuable social function, by bringing people together in a darkened room, to enjoy themselves in silence, gazing at a spinning wheel!

And aren't we all, in a very real sense, just players on the Great Wheel of Fortune, wondering whether we will land on the black or the red, the odd or the even, the gay or the straight?

And when we have all had our 'harmless night of fun', will we go home having 'filled our boots'?

Gamblers are welcome in the parish but not smokers! As seen by local artist Mr de la Nougerede

Or will we perhaps return home penniless, to watch our wives and children starve to death and then take the only honourable way out by jumping in the path of an Intercity train (if there are any!)?

I'm only joking, of course, because I know that here in St Albion's we are sufficiently adult to ensure that any gambling is conducted only in a responsible manner, so that no one will lose any money.

Furthermore, Mrs Jowell has arranged with Messrs Corleone and Capone that a very large percentage of any profits they may make (possibly as much as 2 percent) will be handed back to the parish to supplement church funds and to provide pensions for the less needy members of the community, following Mr Brown's frankly somewhat incompetent handling of our finances, due to his recurring mental disability (no offence, Gordon!).

Yours,

Tony

Text For The Week

"Greater love hath no man than that he lays down other people's lives for his friend"

Epistle of Tony to the Neo-Corinthians

A Message Of Thanks From The Rev. Dubya Bush Of The Church Of The Latter-Day Moremen

Brothers and Sisters in St Albion's, praise be to your good pastor, the Rev. Terry Bloom, who is once again courageously alone in choosing to give me his unflagellating support in my ongoing crusade against the forces of the Evil One, eg that lily-livered, flip-flopping, liberal-loving, atheistical abortionist and homosexual John Kerry. Only your man Timmy has taken to his heart the concept of loyalitude. He has come to see that there could be no greater disloyality than not doing what I say. Hallelujah! Bring 'em on!

 Rev. Dubya, his mark

 Parish Postbag

A Very Important Letter from Mrs Barbara Follett

Dear Sir,

It is surely no concern of anyone in the parish where I choose to live or who pays for my flat in Asquith Grove. I have very important duties in the parish, which mean that I must have a pied-à-terre near the church (which obviously must be paid for out of parish funds, as is only right and proper), and the fact that I have a modest 19-bedroom mansion up the road is quite irrelevant.

> *Yours,*
> *Mrs Barbara Follett,*
> *(Whichever of my various homes I happen to be in at the time)*

(The Editor reserves the right to print in full any letter which shows up its author in a bad light, particularly if they and their partner happen to have fallen out with the vicar. D. Hill, Editor.)

Women's Groups

Mrs Blears gave a very interesting talk, proving that 90 percent of mothers had been beaten up by their partners during pregnancy.

She argued that it was time for all prospective fathers to be forced by law to register themselves as abusers before attempting to make a woman pregnant.

This would make it easier to arrest them during ante-natal classes. There was a vote of thanks from the ladies and Mrs Jowell then organised a 'responsible' tombola, in which everyone lost their money, but not very much.

Glory, Glory Hallelujah!!!

That has to be the message this week, as we all rejoice in the good news from our brethren in America!

Our good friend, the Rev. Dubya, has been reanointed to serve as Supreme Pastor of all the Morons in the United States of America!

Good news indeed for all of us here in St Albion's, who have derived such inspiration from this great spiritual leader of our time!

And how privileged we are that, amid all the excitement and 'hullabaloo' surrounding his historic reappointment, the Rev. Dubya has agreed to contribute a personal message to all his friends in St Albion's.

From The Office Of The Chief Moron, The White House of the Lord, Washington J.C.

Dear Morons,

Praise the Lord for giving us this great victory over the forces of darkness and evilitude!

Hallelujah! His hand is mighty in lifting up his servant (that's me, folks!) and casting down the hosts of Midian (that's Kerry, guys!) with all the fornicators, sodomites, flip-flop girly men and atheistical abortion-lovers!

And now, having given us this great deliverance, the Lord is sending us forward in our crusade against the Evil One!

And, lo, the trumpet shall sound, and the city of Fallujah shall be laid waste, as was the city of Jericho in bygone Israel-land!

Doesn't that lift your hearts, brothers and sisters? And where next will the sword of righteousness fall in our mission to bring peace and harmony to all the peoples of the earth?

Tremble, o ye coyotes, at the mighty name of Dubya!

For, in the words of Brother Schwarzenegger of the Grand Order of the Terminators, yea I am back!

Sister Condy and Brother Rumsfeld join me in thanking you all for your support and your prayers, which the Lord in his wisdom has heartened unto, even 50-million-fold!

> *Way to go! Bring it on! Hallelujah!*
> *Yours with the Moron Majority,*
> *Rev. Dubya*

Help spread the Good News by posting this letter in your window or passing it on to a fellow Moron.

Printed and published by The Friends Of The Tabernacle, C/o the Hallelujahburton Group

Parish Postings

CONGRATULATIONS to Mrs Jay on her new appointment to our Committee For Standards in Parish Life. No one could be better qualified to root out sleaze and nepotism than Mrs Jay, whose father the Rev. Callaghan was, of course, one of our most-respected incumbents, and who older parishioners will remember appointed her husband as head of our mission in America. She is also, of course, a very old friend of our present vicar, and helped set up a charity to help him when he was a young curate, the Help The Blind Trust. She was also for a while Matron-in-Charge of the St Albion's Sunset Home for Retired Gentlefolk, where she did sterling work getting rid of a lot of the inmates, and releasing them back into the community. So, best of luck to Margaret, as she roots out all that shady business that we all so disapprove of.

THE EIGHTH DEADLY SIN: **GAMBLING**
by The Vicar

In last week's newsletter some readers may have been surprised by the headline given to my article, "God's Gift Of Gambling", in which I appeared to argue that to have slot machines in the south transept and a roulette wheel in the crypt would enrich the spiritual life of the parish.

This was due to an unfortunate typographical error by Mrs Jowell, when she was composing my article, which somehow caused the word 'not' to be omitted from a number of key sentences.

For example, when I apparently wrote "every right-thinking person must be in favour of a massive extension of gambling", I, of course, meant "not in favour". And when I appeared to say "anyone who opposes my proposals is a snob", I, of course, meant "is not a snob".

I'll put my hand up to this one and say, hey, Mrs Jowell was wrong! And I have asked Mr Birt, our systems expert, to take a look at the vicarage computer and see if he can find a way of ensuring that this sort of silly mistake will never happen again. Thanks, John! T.B.

Women's Groups

We are very fortunate to be able to welcome the Vicar's wife, Mrs Cherie Booth, next month when she will give a talk on "How to Give Talks in America". Mrs Booth will be explaining how to supplement the family income by trading on your husband's name and she will tell us amusing anecdotes about eating breakfast in the vicarage. Anyone lucky enough to get a ticket for this – they are going for only £300 each – will learn what the Vicar thinks about *Golden Grahams* and why he prefers *Honey Nut Loops*!

WARNING: Mrs Booth has asked us to make clear that anyone who alleges that on her recent lecture tour of the USA she was in any way critical of or disrespectful to her husband's friend the Rev. Dubya, Pastor-in-Chief of the Church of the Latter-Day Morons, will be liable to receive a writ and a claim for damages for the infringement of her human rights. This, she points out, could result in an award of not less than £1 million and/or a sentence of life imprisonment commuted to death.

✝ *To Remember In Your Prayers*

● May we all particularly remember at this time our good friend Geoff Hoon, who has served so loyally and so long on the Iraq Mission sub-committee of the PCC. In recent days, Geoff has not been very well, and has been saying things that he would have done better to keep quiet about. Give him strength to be more discreet about important decisions that the Vicar has already made but is wisely keeping to himself. May Geoff remember that there are other members of our congregation who could perform his parish duties just as well, if not better than himself. T.B.

ST ALBION PARISH NEWS

26th November 2004

Hullo,

And as Christmas gets ever nearer by the day, our thoughts inevitably turn once again to the message of the angels – *Peace on Earth.*

I know some cynical people these days think that it's just a dream. "That's all pie in the sky, vicar", they say to me.

Well, I'm here to tell them something very different! I wonder whether any of the children can tell me who is the Very Important Person I travelled several thousand miles to see last week?

No, it wasn't Father Christmas, Humvee! That's right, Rashid, it was the Rev. Dubya, from the Church of the Latter-Day Morons!

And aren't you proud that your vicar was the very first person in the whole world that the Rev. Dubya wanted to see, after his historic re-anointment by the millions of Morons all over America!

I felt truly humbled as I stood side by side with this great spiritual leader of our time in the famous White House Tabernacle, to hear him say, "I salute Pastor Blair of England-Land as a really straight kind of guy, who is prepared to support our great crusade against the Evil One and stand up for what I believe at all times. Hail to you, steadfast vicar from across the pond!"

I have to say that I was deeply moved to hear these very sincere words from a true man of God!

But I haven't brought this up just to boast about the Rev. Dubya's very kind words about me! No, the really important message he gave to the world, thanks to the advice that I was able to give him during the five minutes when we were alone together, was his determination over the next four years to bring lasting peace to all mankind!

"Look," he told us, "what has happened to the cities of the plain in Iraq-land. Is not Fallujah laid waste with fire and brimstone, even that peace may be brought to all those that dwell therein?"

And now, having solved the problems of Iraq, I was able to persuade the Rev. Dubya to turn his spiritual gaze on the greatest question of all – what are we to do to bring lasting peace to the Holy Land itself?

I shall never forget the moment when the Rev. Dubya turned to me and said, "I give you my solemn pledge, Toby, that when Sister Condy, Brother Rumsfeld and myself are gathered together in prayer in the Tabernacle of the Morons, we will place the Holy Land-land at the very centre of our prayerful agenda."

You couldn't be more decisive than that, could you? And what better proof that the special relationship between Rev. Dubya and myself can bring truly lasting fruits for all of us!

I would only say that when that great day comes I don't want people saying, "Vicar, it's all thanks to you that the people of the Middle East have learned to live in peace."

No, I want the Rev. Dubya to be given real credit for having had the wisdom to heed my counsel at this historic time!

Someone to whom, I am sorry to say, no credit is due at all is Cardinal Chirac, our French opposite number, who has recently been over in St Albion's, supposedly to mark 100 years of close friendship between our two parishes.

The Cardinal made himself extremely disagreeable, by telling me over tea in my own vicarage that I had wasted my time going to see Rev. Dubya, and that I was making a fool of myself by supporting his ridiculous crusade, which had only made things worse!

Furthermore he didn't drink his tea, and rudely interrupted our talk by playing on the floor with little Leo, so that he could tell everyone afterwards that he "got more sense out of baby Leo than I did from his father".

I try to like most people, as you know, but I have to say that when the Cardinal left the vicarage, I had to ask Mr Milburn to go round with an air-freshener to get rid of the lingering smell of garlic and over-ripe cheese.

Brother Rumsfeld sometimes overstates his case but when he describes our snooty French friend as a "cheese-eating surrender monkey" I think he may have had a point!

Yours,

Tony

VIEW FROM ABROAD

– a message from the former Churchwarden

Is it not time to draw a line and move on from the silly and petulant arguments between members of the PCC? I am thinking in particular of the Parish Treasurer Mr Brown whose bitterness and rancour seem to know no bounds. Just because I pointed out how useless he is at his job (don't mention the deficit anyone or Gordy will have one of his hissy fits!) he seems to have taken it personally. Honestly, what an old queen! He really should grow up and try and concentrate on his job rather than making unpleasant remarks about me behind my back. We all know what this is all about, don't we? Just because all those years ago I said Tony would make a better vicar than Gordon! Well, we've certainly rattled her cage, haven't we?

For heaven's sake, dear, get a life!

Yours,

Peter Mandelson,
Rue des Matelots,
Bruxelles.

A special performance of Les Miserables at the Parish Hall was a great success!

Working Men's Club

Mr Prescott writes:

I am glad to say that, following my personal interventing with our GP Dr Reid, the parish-wide smoking ban will not apply to the St Albion's Working Men's Club as previously expectorated. This is to ensure the continued support of the less well-off members of our congregation, who had threatened to boycott our services in protest against what they rightly described as "a bunch of do-gooding middle-class tossers trying to spoil our fun".

> Yours fraternally,
> J. Prescott, Hon. Sec.,
> Working Men's Club.

CORRECTION

Mrs Jowell writes:

In the last newsletter it was stated that I was in favour of opening hundreds of super-casinos all over the parish. This was a misprint. I would like to make it clear that I am in favour of only 8 small slot machines, and furthermore that none of these are to be next to the altar, as the newsletter incorrectly suggested.

REMEMBRANCE DAY

There was a very good turnout this year for our annual service of remembrance, to see all the new names which have been added to the war memorial. It was good of Mr Billy Bragg to suggest a more up-to-date version of our traditional hymn, "I vow to thee my country", but sadly his song paid tribute to a number of old-fashioned beliefs which we have long since moved on from – i.e. Socialism.

In the end we used another new version specially written by Mr Bragg's brother Melvyn, in which only one word needed to be changed, replacing "country" with "vicar". T.B.

ST ALBION PARISH NEWS

10th December 2004

Hullo!

And can I say right away that this week has clearly been very difficult for all of us, not least for our good friend Mr Blunkett himself.

But through all these unhappy events, which have been such a talking point around the parish, there has been one shining thread of light, to remind us that however black things sometimes look in life, we can always find a silver lining.

And in the case of Mr Blunkett's misfortunes, what better opportunity could they give us to spell out just what should be the core of our beliefs in the 21st century?

I know some of our older parishioners still want to hark back to the days when members of the PCC were expected to "set an example" by the way they lived their private lives!

In those days, if someone "strayed from the path", as they used to put it, there was a great deal of sanctimonious tut-tutting from certain members of the congregation, and on occasion the "offender" was even asked to give up his position!

Well, thank goodness, those days are long since dead and buried!

In the modern church, we now realise that what someone does in their private life is entirely their own concern.

After all, isn't that exactly what the word 'private' means? Do I have to spell it out – P-R-I-V-A-T-E!

And if you see a door with 'private' written on it, you don't just go barging in, do you?

No, you respect that person's right to do whatever they like behind that closed door, because it is nobody's business but their own!

Well, that's what we're talking about here, in a nutshell!

We've moved on from the days when a lot of sour-faced people used to go around giving lectures on "right" and "wrong".

And what a miserable lot they were in those days!

Today we've realised that what matters – the only thing that matters – is whether someone does their job well!

And, in the case of Mr Blunkett, can anyone argue that he hasn't been the best head of our Neighbourhood Watch we've ever had?

Thanks to his hard work and ceaseless vigilance, we can all now sleep more soundly in our beds with whoever we like!

So here is something we can all really be thankful for! That we've at last been liberated from all those judgemental beliefs of yesteryear!

Goodness me, just imagine what would have happened if all this had taken place in days gone by!

We would have seen poor David being taken out and stoned to death! As for his friend Mrs Quinn, she would probably have been burned at the stake as a witch!

Can anyone honestly put their hand on their heart and say that we want to go back to those days?

I thought not! So let's draw a line under this unhappy business, shall we, and wish David godspeed in his efforts to find lasting happiness by breaking up Mrs Quinn's marriage and getting custody over his illegitimate children!

Yours,

Tony

✴ Christmas Quiz! ✴

Our picture shows a kindly, almost saintly figure, who, at this time of year, gives away generous presents to kiddies, mums, dads, grannies and grandpas out of the kindness of his heart. But who is the old guy in red with the beard? Answers to G. Brown, The Vicarage, St Albion. *(Is this right?)*

CHRISTMAS MESSAGE FROM MR BIRT

 As you know, I have spent the last two years drawing up plans on how to re-engineer the parish infrastructure to make more efficient use of its manpower resources. In simple terms, this means that many of you will not have a job anymore, leaving a rationalised and slimmed-down Parish bureaucracy of one, ie myself.

A Merry Christmas to you all!

Mr Birt

PS. In the picture you will see a sack, which should give you a clue as to what the New Year will bring.

 Parish Postbag

From our Treasurer, Mr Brown

Dear Sir,
With regard to my recent presentation of the parish's annual accounts, which are a stunning testimony to my own prudence, ability and hard work, may I make it clear that my task in trying to balance the books would have been made very much easier had it not been for the Vicar's foolhardy and ill-advised support for the Rev. Dubya and his supposed crusade against the Evil One. As a result of the vicar's reckless gullibility in this regard, the parish is now in debt to the tune of
Yours sincerely

(The Editor reserves the right to shorten all letters from our treasurer when he is in one of his sulks, which incidentally are becoming all too frequent these days! D.H.)

Parish Scenes

(that the vicar does not want to see!)

**No. 94:
The Boxing Day
Service**

Thanks to local artist Mr de la Nougerede for this nightmare vision! D.H.

Christmas Charity Appeal

The vicar has given a pledge that next year he will stamp out the scourge of Aids in Africa for once and for all.

Obviously Tony doesn't need your help because he can do this all on his own. But if you want to show your support for his campaign to free the world of this terrible plague, just fill in the form below and send it to the vicarage.

I . . . .
(fill in name) wish to register my support for all the wonderful work the vicar is doing to rid the world of Aids.

ST ALBION PARISH NEWS

24th December 2004

An open letter to Mr Blunkett, formerly Head of the Neighbourhood Watch

Dear David,

It is with deep regret that I have to accept your resignation from the PCC after we sat in the vicarage and talked over the whole unfortunate affair, friend to friend, parson to parishioner, man to man about to be sacked.

I don't think you'll mind me telling the parish, David, that it was an emotional moment when you gave me a big hug and, for some reason, called me "Mrs Quinn".

But, hey, let's get one thing clear. You have done nothing wrong and you leave with your integrity intact. Which may leave some people wondering "Why did he have to go then?". And I suppose the logical extension to that conundrum is that if you *had* done something wrong, you would have *kept* your job!

It doesn't seem to make sense, but, hey, I'm just a parish vicar, and these are deep mysteries that have baffled greater minds than mine for thousands of years!

For example, St Thomas of Uttley made no mention of you, David, in his great work *De Legova Mysteriosa,* and if he couldn't solve this one, then no one can!

So, let's leave it at that, shall we?

What we know, David, is that, sadly, you have had to go, but the church's message is surely one of forgiveness. I have forgiven you, David, even though you have done nothing wrong, which is why you lost your job. And I'm sure there will come a time when we will all look deep into our hearts, and say, "The Vicar was right – as usual. We must all forgive you".

David, you are innocent of all charges, except the ones where you aren't, but, hey, don't we all make honest mistakes and there is no one more honest than you, David – except me, obviously, which is why I'm admitting honestly that you did nothing wrong.

And since we all believe in the possibility of life after death, doesn't this mean, when translated into modern everyday language, that you, David, should get your job back sometime in the New Year?

So can I conclude by wishing you, Lazarus, I mean David, a very, very Happy Christmas and best wishes to your family whoever and wherever they are.

Your good friend, Tony

The Vicar shows off his proposed design for a new stained glass window (with no stains, of course!) commemorating the life and work of his friend St David of Blunkett, who was martyred by so-called colleagues who put him "in the press" until he cracked, so jealous were they of his sanctity, holiness and innocence. Thanks to local artist Mr de la Nougerede for this charming drawing.

Yuletide Fun!

Provided by members of the PCC.

Q: Why is Mr Blunkett like a turkey?
A: Because he got stuffed at Christmas!
(from Mr Prescott)

Q: Why is Mr Blunkett like a high-speed train?
A: Because he went on the 'fast-track' and hit the buffers! (from Mrs Beckett)

Q: Which member of the PCC likes to pull a cracker?
A: Mr Blunkett (geddit?)! (from Mr Straw)

The Vicar writes: These jokes are, I'm afraid, totally out of order. We all like a bit of harmless fun at Christmas time, but this is not in any way amusing. T.B.

WORLD EXCLUSIVE!

Here is the unabridged text of the sermon our vicar will be preaching on December 25 in the St Albion's Worship Centre

Hullo!

First of all, Cherie and I would like to extend our season's greetings to everyone here this morning, and indeed everyone in the parish, regardless of their race, colour, creed or sexual orientation!

A Very Happy Holiday to you all! Unless of course you are one of those people who prefers to be unhappy, which is, of course, your perfect right and an entirely valid lifestyle option!

Or maybe you don't believe in holidays, which again you are perfectly entitled to do – like my nextdoor neighbour, who is not only unhappy all the time, but never stops working at his figures!

Of course, Gordon is free to choose to work all the hours that God sends (sorry, when I say 'God', of course I mean Allah, the Supreme Being, the Chief Jedi, or whatever belief-system you feel comfortable with at this time of year!).

Good for Gordon, I say! But, let's be honest. All that hard work hasn't exactly made the parish accounts look very healthy, has it?

Still, love your neighbour, that is my motto! And if your neighbour is hard to love, then that's so much more of a challenge, isn't it?

But, hey, aren't we forgetting the real message of Christmas/Eid/Hanukkah/Diwali/Winterval/the Notting Hill Festival?

And what is that message, I hear you ask, Rashid?

Peace on earth, goodwill to men! Isn't that what people used to say in the old days?

Nowadays, of course, we put it rather better, by saying peace on earth (except in certain trouble spots where war is the only option); and goodwill to all persons (which makes clear that we are including women, members of the gay and lesbian communities, and, of course, all those persons of trans-gender status).

But, look, isn't there something a little bit wrong with such a sweeping generalisation?

I am sure when we talk about "goodwill to all persons", we aren't meant to take that as meaning literally *all* persons, are we?

I mean, there are obviously certain categories of persons whom it would be quite wrong for us to feel goodwill towards!

Can any of the children guess who I am thinking of here?

Yes, Ranjit, 'terrorists' – that's a good answer! But it's not quite the one I was thinking of!

What I had in mind was someone beginning with 'B'!

No, Justin, not Mr Blunkett. That's not funny or clever. You can see Mrs Hodge afterwards. And, yes, I thought that would scare you!

No, Justin, come out of the cupboard! I know your father's a lawyer. Just my little joke.

Anyway, we're rather in danger of losing the point of this Yuletide message, aren't we?

The word I was looking for, of course, was 'burglars'!

When we're thinking about all those people in the world who don't deserve any goodwill, then top of the list must surely be 'B-U-R-G-L-A-R-S'. Everyone hates burglars, don't they? And I'd like to make it very clear that I am second to no one in my hatred of burglars!

I know our local solicitor Mr Howard has been going round the parish saying that hating them was *his* idea!

But it wasn't anything to do with him! It was me who pointed out that burglars were becoming a real menace in our society today, and that they should all be shot!

Of course, I don't mean that literally, since guns have very rightly been banned!

But what I *do* mean is that if, for example, you knew that a certain person was determined, come what may, to enter your house, sit at your desk, raid your fridge and make free with your toilet, wouldn't you be entitled to take any measures to stop such a person doing such a thing?

Particularly if you had repeatedly warned this person to keep out of your house and to stop trying to steal your job!

So my message this Christmas is "Gordon, stay on your own side of the wall!". As it says in the Good Book, "This *is* a gun in my pocket, and I'm not pleased to see you" *(The Meditations of Saint Mae of the West)*.

So, thank you all for coming, and I hope when you return home you will richly enjoy your traditional Midwinter Festival meal.

At the vicarage, we'll be having turkey! But if you're having gefilte fish, samosas, nut cutlets or a good old burger and fries, the message of the angels is the same – enjoy!

NATIVITY PLAY

Mrs Jowell writes:

I regret to announce that we cannot afford to stage the nativity play this year since we need the so-called "Theatre Budget" to pay for the new slot machines in the South Transept and the roulette wheel in the crypt. I am sure all parishioners will agree that this is a very wise investment and is what the church is *all* about!

The same applies to the craft fair, the art show and the various other "cultural" (!) activities which have had to be sacrificed in favour of the Church Gambling Project. But I am sure we all agree they will not be missed, since they belong to another elitist and frankly bygone era. Mrs T.J.

A STRONGLY WORDED NOTE FROM MR PRESCOTT OF THE WORKING MEN'S CLUB

A lot of people in the parish have criticised the Vicar quite unreservedly for staying on holiday when there are urgent matters requiring his immediate detention at home. This is totally unfair and unwarrantied. The Vicar and his good lady deserve a break as much as anyone else and it is quite disappropriate for people to circumcise them for having a nice time on the beach in a swanky resort for nobs whilst some people are left to do all the work as per bloody usual with no thanks at the end of it!

Let me insure you all that actually things have been working very smoothly here in the Vicar's abstention thanks to yours truly being in charge.

In fact a number of people have been kind enough to say to me that if the Vicar decided to stay in Egypt forever sunning himself for health reasons then no one would do a better job than me (Thanks Mrs Prescott!).

So let that be an end to this malicious criticism of the Vicar and let's all concentrate on making this a great new year for St Albion's.

Yours in charge,
John Prescott

PS. Here is a transcript of an interview given to Mr Snow from our local hospital radio station down the phone from the Vicar – just to reassure the more scepticised amongst you that all is fine!

"There is no need for anyone to panic, Jon, as I am in constant touch with everyone around the world all the time. To be honest, Jon, the fact that I am on holiday makes no difference at all since I might as well be at my desk, that is how in touch I am. So don't ask me if I am in touch, Jon, because I'm more in touch than if I was in my office with all those other things to distract me. No, I'm doing a great job here which is why I'll be flying home as soon as possible. Happy New Year to all your listeners."

The Vicar collects together all the "black sheep" of the parish and brings them back into the fold! As seen by local artist Mr de la Nougerede

JANUARY BOOK SALE!!

Due to the huge success of Cherie's wonderful book Ten Famous Vicars' Wives (by Mrs Booth, with additional material supplied by Mrs Bragg, although obviously Cherie wrote the lion's share!), we are happy to be able to announce a special offer of signed copies of this must-read best-seller at only 30p per copy. As Cherie herself points out, this is terrific value, and we hope that as many of you as possible will come along to our January 'Bring and Buy Sale' (you bring the money and then you buy the book!). Mr Milburn will be keeping a record of all parishioners who have felt themselves unable to support this very good cause! T.B.

CORRECTION:

Some parishioners seem to have got the wrong impression from our last newsletter that Mr Blunkett has somehow "lost his job " on the PCC. Nothing could be further from the truth. As we all know, David has been working very hard on all our behalfs in recent years, and just before Christmas he came to me saying that he was very tired (or "shagged out" as he put it, in his direct Northern dialect!) and could he therefore have my permission to take a 'sabbatical' (from the Greek 'sabbatikos', 'sabba' meaning slap, and 'tikkos', tickle). David plans to take a few months off, to "recharge his batteries", and will be working from home (his own, or possibly someone else's!). But I am sure you will be delighted to know that David will, in due course, be rejoining our team ministry, with a new job description, possibly in a very senior position indeed! Well done, David, great to have you back! (Not that you've been away!) T.B.

EXCLUSIVE
From the Holy Land at Christmas!!
Only in the St Albion parish newsletter!!

Hullo!

And let me say how thrilled I am to be writing these words from a place which we all think about every Christmas holiday!

I mean, of course, the Holy Land, which for far too many years has been associated in our minds with wars and conflicts!

Many good men over the years (and of course women!) have tried to bring peace to this troubled land, including my very good ex-friend the Rev. Jefferson Clintstone of the Church of the Seven-Day Fornicators, and my current good friend, the Rev. Dubya of the Church of the Latter-Day Morons.

But, sad to say, every single one of them failed, which means that the people of this land are still looking for that long-promised saviour who will sort the whole thing out once and for all, so that you can all draw a line under it and move on!

As it was written, "And one shall come who shall be called Wonderful, the Privy Councillor, the Prince of Peace".

Well, I was pondering on those wise words a little while back, taken from the Book of the Lord Levyticus, and I thought to myself, "Hey! That rings something of a bell!".

And without wanting to blow my own trumpet, I realised that there is probably only one person around at the moment who could honestly say, "I'm the man for the job!".

So that's why I decided that this Christmas, instead of just sitting around at home, watching television and eating too many mince pies (no offence to our friend, Mr Prescott!), I should get out here to the Middle East and knock a few heads together, until they come to their senses! (No offence, obviously!)

My plan was simple! I would invite the two sides to sit round the table with me back in St Albion's, and we would jolly well sit there all night, if necessary, until we'd found the solution that everybody wants! And that's precisely what's going to happen! Except that, unfortunately, one side has told me that they are not going to come to the talks. And neither is the other.

But that doesn't mean to say that we won't achieve anything! On the contrary, I think it marks a really positive start! At least both sides are totally agreed on one thing, and that must be good news!

As we say over here, "Shalom" – which is the local way of saying "Happy New Year"!

© *T. Blair 2005*

ST ALBION PARISH NEWS

21st January 2005

Hullo!

And I don't mind admitting that the start of this year has been a highly invigorating (if somewhat humbling) experience!

Over the years, I've got rather used to standing up in the pulpit and preaching to all of you.

So when the tables were turned at our recent special meeting in the Church Hall, it was something of a shock to have to listen to all of you lecturing me!

And, as I sat there while you told me that our treasurer Mr Brown and I should stop our constant bickering, goodness me – did I feel chastened and humbled? But also annoyed!

Because, let's be fair, when it comes to the bickering, we all know who started it, don't we?

And it wasn't your vicar!

Who was it who apparently said "I can't believe a word of what the vicar says about anything"?

Not a very nice thing to say, is it?

No wonder Mr Brown, sitting on the platform at the meeting with his arms folded and a gloomy expression on his face, said nothing!

As it is written in the *Book of Proverbs*, "Silence is Gordon"!

And let's not forget who it was who carefully arranged his talk about Africa months before, so that it would clash with the talk on Asia that I had organised that very morning, to take place at the same time.

So there we were, with the ridiculous situation of Mr Brown down at the Scout Hut with no one to listen to him – and me in the church, with a packed congregation applauding my deeply compassionate sermon!

And that's meant to be my fault? Puh-leease!!!

So, let's get this whole thing clear, shall we?

It's time to put all this talk about bickering behind us, and move on! Particularly gloomy Gordon!

Everyone is totally agreed about this. There is now 100 percent unity in the parish on the moving on from the bickering issue (apart from Gordon!).

So, I'm going to move on anyway, and Gordon can do what he likes!

I've got a job to do, and one, I would like to make it clear, which I never agreed to hand over to anyone else! Why would I?

That would be stupid, when everyone is begging me to stay on, wouldn't it?

So can I just say here, before I say anything else, that I would like to offer my sincere condolences to all those who lost loved ones in the various recent natural disasters, both at home and abroad.

I think we can all agree that these have very much put into perspective such trivial matters as people making their silly little points about the way I run the parish!

Yours (more in anger than in sorrow!),

Tony

Village Panto
'Spinderella!'

Another cracking production by the St Albion Players, which had the audience falling about. We particularly loved the scene where the ugly sister (was that Mr Brown doing a fine grumpy turn?) told Prince Charming (the Vicar on fine form!) that he didn't believe a thing he said. "Oh yes, you do," said Tony. "Oh no, I don't," said Gordon. And so it went on for hours – until long after the audience had left. Can't wait for next year's 'Blair Babes In The Woods'. A.M.

Helping the homeless

As you will all be aware, the Vicar and his good lady have generously agreed to rent out their beatiful new house in Ratrun Square, as their contribution to helping the homeless. They have now, even more generously, agreed to reduce the rent they are asking to an even more affordable level – from £20,000 a week to a rock bottom £19,000.

If you would like the chance to snap up this luxurious home, with easy access to a number of delightful Lebanese restaurants, Iranian chemists and a branch of the Al Qaeda Bank, apply at once to Messrs Feiner de Smith (Lovely Properties 'R' Us). A.M.

Parish Support Line

Has your faith in the Vicar been shaken by recent terrible events?

Some people in the parish have been asking in recent weeks – if he is so "omnipotent", how can he let these awful things happen?

There's no easy answer to this. Some people say that the Vicar gave Gordon "free will" to do whatever he wanted. So he can't be held to blame!

Others say it's not so simple. The Vicar moves in a mysterious way and it is not for us to attempt to fathom his mysterious purposes!

If you are one of those whose faith has been put to the test, why not seek expert counselling by ringing Mr Milburn on the vicarage support line, where you can hear a special recorded explanation of how you have got it wrong!

(There is no need to leave contact details, because Mr Mandelson has passed on his address book, so Mr Milburn knows where you live!)

Salve!

A BIG ST ALBION'S WELCOME into the fold to Mr Jackson of whom none of you had heard until this week!

"I have been converted," he told everyone at his induction service. "All these years I have been walking in darkness and now I have seen the light."

Mr Jackson used to belong to the obscure Transylvanian cult led by Mr Howard, our local solicitor, who believe that they are "undead" and that one day they will be reincarnated and come back to life.

He now accepts that this is silly, and he realises that the Vicar represents the only path to salvation.

As the Good Book says, "There is more rejoicing in one sinner who repents than 99 boring members of the PCC who do what they are told"! T.B.

Parish Tsunami Appeal

An anonymous benefactor has very kindly and generously donated a whole binliner-full of old children's toys to our local charity shop. The value of these toys has been professionally valued at a staggering £8.50! Well done, Mrs Blair!

A VERY IMPORTANT ANNOUNCEMENT

Some confusion has recently arisen over who does what at the top of our parish organisation.

I have therefore appointed Mr Birt as Chief Parish Co-ordinator. This is a new post, the holder of which will exercise many of the responsibilities formerly shouldered by other members of the PCC (no offence, guys, it's just a case of 'moving on'!).

St Albion's Team Ministry
HOW IT NOW WORKS

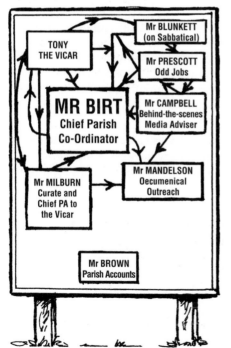

As you know, I have become increasingly reliant on John's advice on how to simplify the procedures of parish administration, whether it be the drawing up of the flower roster, re-organisation of our system for the dispensing of coffee and biscuits after Sunday services or the allocation of priority parking spaces for the disabled and for senior members of the PCC in the church car park (formerly the graveyard).

This is why I have now asked John to move into the vicarage on a permanent basis – up in the attic, so he can do his "blue sky thinking".

So over to you, John, for a bit of your "structural re-engineering"!!! T.B.

ST ALBION PARISH NEWS

4th February 2005

Hullo!

And this week I'm writing to you all from Switzerland, where I have had the privilege of addressing church leaders from all over the world, in one of the most important oecumenical gatherings ever held.

We met in the beautiful city of Davos nestling in the shadow of the Alps, which in the days before global warming used to be covered in snow.

Not that you can put everything down to global warming, of course, as I was quick to tell all the delegates who had come from every corner of the world to hear what I had to say!

Like so many things in life, I explained to them, it's not that easy!

No, my main message at the interfaith forum was to try to dispel some of the misconceptions which have grown up around my friend the Rev. Dubya!

For some reason, a lot of people lately have been accusing the Rev. Dubya of being something of a "warmonger", for his great crusade to rid the world of evil!

And I have to say that some of those people were here at the meeting, including Monsignor Chirac and Pastor Schroeder.

Hey, I have the greatest respect for both of these spiritual leaders of our age. But, honestly, you would have to go far to find anyone more childish and ignorant than these two!

As I tried to tell them, I know Rev. Dubya very much better than they do – in fact probably better than anyone else in the world!

Wasn't it me after all, who he rang up and said, "Tony, you're going to support me on this great crusade whether you like it or not".

And haven't I on so many occasions broken bread with the Rev. Dubya in the Great Hall of the Tabernacle of the Morons?

Yea, I have been permitted to join in prayer with Sister Condy and Brother Rumsfeld, as they entreated the Lord to grant them "war in our time", and to agree that they were righteous in all they had done to pursue that goal!

I know the Rev. Dubya, and I know that, since he was anointed by his grateful congregation to serve them for another four years as the Chief Moron, he is very much a changed man!

No longer is he a warmonger, as our fainthearted European brethren try to make out.

Not of course that he was ever a warmonger. He was merely a mighty warrior in the cause of peace!

Haven't they read the Good Book, where Our Lord lays down his doctrine of the pre-emptive strike, in those inspiring words "If your neighbour looks as though he may be about to strike you on the cheek, make sure you hit him first" *(St Paul Wolfowitz's Letter to the Neo-Corinthians)*?

No, I can personally vouch for the fact that my friend Dubya has been very much misunderstood by almost everyone.

But I hear people say, "If you're such a good friend of his, why can't you get him to see sense when it comes to the great moral issues of our time, such as global warming, world poverty and the Middle East?"

But, hey, that's not how you relate with someone of the stature of Rev. Dubya!

No, you don't just tell him he's wrong. You listen attentively to his point of view, and then you very carefully, step by step, spell out to him exactly why you agree with him!

That's how it works! That's what we call a true partnership – working together as one to achieve his common goal!

No wonder the delegates here in Davos (from the Greek "Dav", meaning "free" and "os", meaning a winter holiday) repeatedly gave me a standing ovation in the middle of my speech, as they got up from their chairs to leave the room!

Yours,

Tony

The Vicar tells Mr Clarke, from the Neighbourhood Watch, about a suspicious figure in the parish who is out to get him! As seen by local artist Mr de la Nougerede

Homes for the homeless

We are happy to report a success in the Vicar's ongoing campaign to help out the disabled and the unemployed, who are often particularly vulnerable to the threat of homelessness. Mr "B" (David has particularly asked us not to give his full name) lost his job just before Christmas, through no fault of his own. He was therefore faced with the prospect of having to lose his home and "sleep rough" (believed to be a reference to Mrs Fortier). But thanks to the Vicar's personal initiative, Mr "B" has been allowed to stay on in his home, funded by the parish, until such a time as he gets his job back, which will be in May!

St Albions's Primary School

Mr Twiggy writes:

I would like to thank everyone who helped to make our special Gay, Lesbian and Transgender Awareness Week such a success! The 5-year-olds in the reception class particularly enjoyed our revised Shakespeare production, "Romeo and Julian". Also much enjoyed by the older pupils (7-8-year-olds) was our visit to The Florence Nightingale Dyke Experience in Soho's colourful Old Compton Street. And I haven't even got room to mention my own combination, a history lecture with slides on "Ladyboys Through The Ages"! S.T.

MISSION TO AFRICA

The Vicar would like to make it plain that the mission to Africa is his responsibility, and his alone.

He has been preaching about how he will abolish poverty and Aids for a very long time, and therefore does not appreciate it when other people in the parish come along late in the day and try to earn a few "Brownie points" (no clues there!) by having their photograph taken swanning around Africa pretending to show concern for people's problems, and kissing any children they could get their hands on! This is the kind of thing that should be left to a fully-qualified man of the cloth and missionary, not some Johnny-come-lately who ought to be staying at home doing the job he's meant to do, i.e. trying to get his sums to add up which they so obviously don't!

When it comes to compassion and heartwarming concern for others, I think I can honestly say I'm the man for the job. T.B.

£ CHERIETY APPEAL £

The Vicar's wife will shortly be flying to Australia to lend a hand in raising money for a number of her favourite causes, one of which is the Blair Foundation Fund which helps retired vicars and their wives to live in greater comfort in an agreeable period residence in Ratrun Place (still vacant for letting, rental reduced to an amazing £17,000 per week. Apply c/o Vicarage at once).

Cherie will be addressing gatherings of important local ladies about life in the Vicarage in the following major cities:

Goolagong, Digger's Bottom, Kangarooni Falls, Sheila Springs, Bradman Rock, Kellytown, Alan Botney Bay, Didgeridoo, Abo's End... and many more.

Tickets still available from Booth Charity Vacations, c/o the Vicarage.
£13,000 per ticket (flight not included).

Book now to avoid disappointment.

Mr O'Brien writes:

A special "hello" or rather "halal" to all our Muslim readers whom we are delighted to welcome into our flock. We are very keen for you all to join in the life of St Albion by voting for the Vicar when the PCC elections come round. We know that you Muslims are sensible people, far too sensible to be fooled by the likes of local solicitor Michael Howard who as you all know is well, not one of us, or indeed, one of you and therefore cannot be trusted on important local issues like Palestine. Allah be with you!

Mr O'Brien,
Co-Chair Muslims For The Vicar Committee,
c/o The Vicarage.

YOUTH CLUB

For those of you who missed the Vicar's exciting interview with June Swoon on the St Albion sixth form youth FM radio station, here are the highlights:

What is our favourite band?

Whoever young people like... er, it says here Grace Kelly, oh no that's the answer to the next question.

Who was your pin-up when you were at school?

Ruth Kelly. I really fancied her... oh, no, er... I mean Gene Kelly... oh, sorry, Kelly Holmes.

Have you ever given your wife any flowers?

Franz Ferdinand... or is it Rio Ferdinand? I'm afraid I've got to "wing it daddyo" as you say, isn't it cool in here? *Ciao baby.*

ST ALBION PARISH NEWS

18th February 2005

HEY, WE'RE SORRY!!!

What's the hardest word to say in the English language?
I expect some of the children will know the answer!
It's 'sorry', isn't it?

But let me tell you, it's not so hard when you really *are* sorry!
You're not just saying it. You're feeling it and meaning it!

Which is where your vicar comes in. Because I recently had to
say 'sorry' in public, for something really bad.

Something really nasty that had been done to some good,
innocent people who'd been put in prison for something they
hadn't done!

You can't get much worse than that, can you?

If ever there was something that cried out for the word 'sorry' in
huge letters, this was it!

But, hey, don't get me wrong. This was a long time ago, and this
terrible thing happened under a previous vicar of this parish.

I was only a young theology student at the time, trying to make
sense of the world, as young people do, strumming my guitar with
my youth group, The Third Way (although there were four of us!).

But, and this is the big 'but', even though it had nothing
whatever to do with me, I'm big enough to say 'sorry' for it!

And I'm not going to stop there! I'm also happy to go on record
issuing a public apology on behalf of another previous vicar, the
Rev. Major, for losing all the church's money on a never-to-be-
forgotten Wednesday afternoon, when the parish treasurer of the
time, Mr Lamont, bet everything on a horse called ERM which fell
over at the first fence!

You won't hear the Rev. Major apologising for such an
unforgiveable act of irresponsibility!

But, I'm afraid, when we were looking through the parish
archives the other day, at the suggestion of my friend Mr
Campbell, there it all was in black and white – just what a
recklessly stupid vicar the Rev. Major was!

As for Mr Lamont, the presence in the church safe of a pile of
receipts from our local branch of Thresher's might suggest that
there were other reasons why Mr Lamont's judgement was so poor
on that occasion!

But, obviously, I do not want to embarrass Mr Lamont by digging up his private problems!

The important thing is that we should open up all our parish records for public inspection, which is why any parishioner can now access any event that took place in the history of the parish, right up to as recently as May 3 1997!

That's saying something, isn't it?

So there we have it. I have absolutely no hesitation in putting my hand on my heart and apologising for any mistakes that were made under previous vicars!

Fortunately, the vicars of the future will be spared having to face up to such a tough challenge because, let's be honest, there's nothing that's happened in the past eight years that will need an apology from anyone!

Older parishioners will remember that much-loved old hymn 'Who's Sorry Now?'.

Well, *I* am! I don't mind telling you how much better I feel when I've apologised for someone else's mistakes!

In fact, I've written an updated version of that old chorus, which we're all going to sing at this week's Sunday evening service:

 We're sorry, we're sorry,
We're really, really sorry.
That's why we all don't mind saying
That we're all sorry now!

Words and music T. Blair.

A Personal Triumph

 I am sure everyone in the parish would like to join me in congratulating the courageous individual whose astonishing achievements have recently been making headlines all round the world. Battling against all manner of storms, defying the most fearful odds, this lone fighter has confounded the critics and sailed safely into harbour, as I always said I would! T.B.

☺ *Welcome Back* ☹

We are very pleased to have Mr Campbell back in the parish team on a full-time basis, as our Communications Outreach Coordinator.

As you may remember, Mr Campbell had a bit of a "breakdown" last summer, and I told him that he could take some time off. I said to him, "Alastair, take as long as you like, and you can come back just as soon as you're feeling better."

Unfortunately he has not responded to his medication, which means that he is still suffering from what the doctors apparently call "Tourette's Syndrome". This is a very sad medical condition, which means that the patient, through no fault of his own, suddenly gives vent to a continual stream of obscenities. Naturally, this might cause offence to some older people. But it's important that no one takes this personally. If he comes up to you in the street and calls you a "f***ing t**t" he doesn't mean it. In fact, he doesn't even know he's saying it. It's just Alastair's way of being friendly!

Scenes from Parish Life

"The welcoming back of the unrepentant sinner!"
As seen by local artist Mr de la Nougerede

That's why we've given him his job back, so that he can work through some of his problems and focus his undoubted talents on working for the good of the parish.

So, if you get an email in the middle of the night calling you something unpleasant and saying that your head is going to be kicked in, I hope you will have the good sense to forget about it! Let us all try to remember that Mr Campbell is a very sick man, with all kinds of personality disorders, and it behoves us all to treat him with compassion!

And I don't mind admitting that sometimes, in spite of his illness, Mr Campbell does sometimes get it spot on when he gives somebody an earful! So I personally am very grateful to him for agreeing to come back to the Vicarage to help me out in the relaunch of the "good ship St Albion" as it sets out on its third epic voyage! Alastair has made a great start by going out at night with his spray-can and writing "Mr Howard Is A Pig" on the bus-shelter! T.B.

Cut-out-'n'-Keep

The Vicar's Six Pledges

❶ Happiness for all

❷ A nice home for everyone

❸ Tidy streets

❹ Lovely hospitals

❺ Bright and cheerful classrooms

❻ Sunny weather

Tombola News

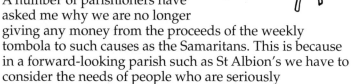

Mrs Jowell writes:

A number of parishioners have asked me why we are no longer giving any money from the proceeds of the weekly tombola to such causes as the Samaritans. This is because in a forward-looking parish such as St Albion's we have to consider the needs of people who are seriously disadvantaged, rather than just suicidal.

That is why the bulk of our funds this year will go to the St Albion's Ethnic and Disabled Sex Workers Collective, who have submitted imaginative plans for a wheelchair-accessible brothel on the High Street, next to the public library. T.J.

A warning from Mr Mandelson, our former churchwarden, who is now heading up our Oecumenical Outreach programme in Brussels

As you may remember, I know where you all live! In particular, I know where Mr Humphrys, the presenter of BBC Radio Albion's 'Good Morning Albion!' show, lives! Mr Humphrys has been persistently negative in his attitude towards our European Outreach project. And, not only that, he has been extremely disrespectful towards the Vicar, not to mention my new good friend Mr Campbell. Mr Humphrys is of course perfectly entitled to say whatever he likes. But, should he turn up one morning and find the whole building has burned to the ground, he should realise that he has only himself to blame!

He should remember my famous motto – *"I'm a lighter, not a quitter!"*

P. Mandelson,
612 Rue des Matelots, Bruxelles.

OFFICIAL HAND-MOVEMENTS TO USE WHEN SINGING YOUR FAVOURITE CHORUS IN CHURCH

He's got the whole world...

...in his hands!

He's got the whole world...

...in his hands!

He's got the whole world...

...in his hands!

The vicar's got us...

...in his hands!!

He's got the whole wide world...   *...in his hands!*

He's got you and me brother...   *...in his hands!*

He's got you and me sister...   *...in his hands!*

And we're all safe...   *...in the vicar's hands!!*

NOW YOU TOO CAN JOIN IN THE FUN!! ©T.BLAIR

ST ALBION PARISH NEWS

4th March 2005

Hullo!

You've all probably by now seen the handsome new signboard which Mr Milburn has put up outside the church "Forwards Not Backwards"!

But I wonder how many of you have taken a few minutes off to meditate on what it really means!

Because, judging by the way some people talk, they would be only too happy to go backwards rather than forwards, which is obviously ridiculous!

And let me give you one very good example of why going backwards is the daftest thing we could do!

In the olden days you weren't allowed to be locked up in your own house without any evidence!

In the 21st Century, doesn't that seem totally absurd? That sort of thing was all very well for the days of bows and arrows, Kings and Knights, Magna Cartas and Habeas Corpuses – but honestly.

We really have to be a bit more modern than that, don't we? Just think how many superstitious beliefs people used to have in the Middle Ages.

They even used to believe in something called 'trial by jury'! Doesn't that sound like something from some fusty old textbook, probably written down on parchment, whatever that was!

Imagine it. They thought that they could just go out into the street and round up 12 ordinary people, none of whom were members of the PCC, and that they could decide whether someone had done wrong or not!

How much more sensible it is to leave all that sort of thing to the experts like Mr Clarke of the Neighbourhood Watch.

Forwards not backwards, you see!

Which brings me to my fifth point!

If there's one thing more than anything else which I've seen as my top priority since I took over as your vicar in 1997, it is that I must always put the wellbeing of my parishioners first!

You remember in the Good Book there's a lot of talk about shepherds? Can any of the children tell me what a shepherd is?

No, Rafik, he's not a halal butcher, but near!

Anyone else? Madison, no it's not a type of German dog, although that was a good guess!

No? Well, let me tell you. A shepherd in the old days was a person whose job was to go out into the fields and round up the sheep.

And then, if he was a good shepherd, and looking after their interest, he would bring them back home at night and make sure that they were safely locked up, to protect them from foxes!

Not that I've got anything against foxes, of course, which do a very useful job in their own way, keeping down the numbers of chickens, ducks and lambs!

But the point is, and this is my seventh final point, if you imagine that not all foxes are good, and that some might be 'suicide foxes', trying to sneak in amongst the sheep to kill them all, then you will see why it makes perfect sense to lock up the sheep and let the foxes go about their business free from discrimination.

Or is it the other way round?

Anyway, the important point is that we go forward, not backwards, as I have made clear by writing a rousing new chorus which we shall be singing at next Sunday's evening service.

Forwards, not backwards
That's the way to go
Forwards, not backwards,
Fast not slow.

Forwards, not backwards,
The future, not the past
Forwards, not backwards
Then it's going to last!

Forwards, not backwards
It's the only way, you know!
Forwards, not backwards,
'Ere we go, 'ere we go, 'ere we go!

Tony

Words and music, T. Blair

BRINGING PEACE TO THE HOLY LAND

The vicar's outreach mission to Palestine is going terribly well.

This week there is an unprecedented peace conference in St Albion's bringing together both sides in this long-running conflict except for one of them. Under the chairmanship of the vicar, there is every chance that the one side will agree with itself and real progress will be made. T.B.

Parish Postbag

Mr Brown takes the parish begging bowl to far-off China! As pictured by local artist Mr de la Nougerede

Dear Sir,

As a former incumbent of this parish, I would like to say how not inconsiderably shocked I am to see the collapse in standards under the present incumbent. Oh yes. And the behaviour of his friend Mr Campbell in particular, as he goes round the parish with his spray can writing obscenities on the bus shelter is, to my mind, in no small measure morally repugnant. And as I said to my wife Norma over breakfast

Yours faithfully,

Rev. J. Major (Vicar of Albion's 1990-7) Maastricht Road.

(The Editor reserves the right to cut all letters from former incumbents who've got the nerve to go around preaching about morality when they were shagging the knickers off Mrs Currie. A.C.)

Banns of Marriage

We are happy to publish the Banns of Marriage between Charles Frederick Ponsonby de la Vere Windsor of this parish, and his long-term partner, Miss Camilla Deirdre Delilah Jezebel Parker-Knoll, one-time spinster, also of this parish.

If anyone knows of any more reasons why these two should not be joined in holy matrimony, could they keep them to themselves, as Mr Falconer has had enough trouble with this one as it is.

For parishioners' information, Mr Falconer had made it clear that the Human Rights Act 2005 allows anyone the right to do anything, so long as the vicar approves it. Which in this case I do! T.B.

It was extremely unfortunate that so few parishioners bothered to turn up for the Vicar's Lent Talk on Tuesday. I have therefore decided to reprint his very important message in full, so that all members of our congregation can get it into their thick skulls. Got it, scumbags?

A. Campbell, Acting Editor.

That Talk In Full

Hullo, and it's good to see so many of you here tonight, despite the wintry weather and the fact that the Chelsea game is on the TV! So if the three of you would like to come nearer to the front, I thought we could spend a few minutes looking at two of the most important words in the English language. I've written them up on these cards, so that those of you at the back can see them clearly. Not that there are any of you at the back, because you've all moved forwards.

And that's good too, because, as you know, that's our new parish mission statement: '*Forwards not backwards*'!

So, here are my two words. This first card says 'Freedom', and the other card reads 'Safety'.

And we want both of these things in this life, don't we? It's not a question of either/or. It's more a matter of both/and!

So, let's just look at those two big words, shall we? 'Freedom.' It's a wonderful thing, isn't it? We all want to be free, don't we?

We all want to be free to leave our homes whenever we like. Or make phone calls to our friends. Or send emails. Or have visits from our loved ones.

But, hey, let's bring in our other word, shall we? 'Safety.' Isn't that something else that we're keen on?

Don't we all remember the old saying, "Safety first"? And that's still as true today as it ever was!

And the important thing to realise is that you can't be free unless you are safe. You can't have one without the other. Are you with me? This is where the two big words that we're thinking about finally come together.

And this brings me to my third and final point.

What we want is the freedom to be safe!

Some of the older people in the parish, I know, can't really get their heads round this one!

A lot of the residents in our St Albion's Retirement Home have been muttering lately that nothing is more important than freedom and that somehow I am trying to take it away from them!

Goodness me, some of them really are getting old and suffering from dementia, aren't they?

Not that I want to embarrass them by naming them, but my old friend Mr Lairg was certainly acting very strangely when I saw him the other day staggering out of the Chancellor's Arms at half-past-three in the afternoon!

His face was very red, and he was obviously having difficulty walking in a straight line! No wonder he can't think straight when it comes to those Big Words!

But let's not bring this down to personalities, as some other people have been trying to do!

You haven't come here tonight to hear me being rude about my old friend Derry Lairg, just because he's always had a bit of a weakness for the bottle!

It would be quite wrong of me to dig up old stories about our former parish solicitor, such as the time when he fell asleep in the toilet and was locked into his office all night!

And, dear me, the next morning, when the cleaners found him, he couldn't even remember his own name!

Which brings me to my closing point, which is that if we need the freedom to be safe, we also need the safety to be free!

Next week's Lenten talk will be given by Dr John Reid under the title 'Who Are You Looking At, Jimmy?' Tickets available from Mrs Blears. Let's have a good turn-out, shall we? Or John might get very annoyed and borrow a list of where you all live from our former churchwarden Mr Mandelson.

The Vicar's Mission To Women

Are women in the parish being heard?

The Vicar has decided it's time to go out and listen to what the ladies of St Albion's have to say. This week he will be fulfilling the following engagements:

Monday
The Cosmopolitan Fellowship, Marcelle D'Argy Smith Hall
The Vicar will be answering questions on abortion, sexually-transmitted diseases and foot fetishism.

Tuesday
Women Against The War, Galloway Assembly Rooms
The Vicar will not be answering questions about the war.

Wednesday
Women's Institute Coffee Morning, The Florence Nightingale Suite, Ramada Hotel
The Vicar will be thanking the ladies for the delicious coffee and home-made biscuits.

Thursday
Mothers and Toddlers Group, The Kimberly Quinn Centre
The Vicar will be spelling out the importance of the family and urging more women to go out to work.

Friday
St Albion's Hospital Radio, "Women Matters"
The Vicar will be talking to presenter Jilly Duffer and playing some of his favourite records.

Saturday
Reading Group at Mrs Morris's
The Vicar drops in at the local book group, where the ladies have been reading Cherie Booth's brilliant new best-seller 'Inside The Vicarage – A Woman's View'.

Sunday
Women's Only Service
The Vicar will preach on the text "God The Mother". No hymns.

Announcement

Mr Brown will be making his annual presentation of the parish accounts on Wednesday. We can expect Mr Brown to tell us how well he has done balancing the books and all that sort of thing and, to be honest, some people really can be a bore on their pet subject, can't they? Wasn't there something in the Good Book about hiding your light under a bushell? Gordon, please note! T.B.

Parish Postbag

Dear Sir,

Could I use your columns to thank everyone for all their marvellous messages of support during what has been a very difficult time for me. I would like you all to know that I am now feeling much better than ever and I am ready to resume my duties on the PCC – should the Vicar decide that my humble services are required! May I also thank the Vicar for allowing me to remain in my 'grace-and-favour' residence during my enforced sabbatical.

His charitable response to my predicament makes a marked contrast to some of those spiteful parishioners who have seen fit to judge me and my behaviour in regard to Mrs Quinn.

I repeat that I have acted at all times with the utmost honesty and integrity – qualities that are sadly lacking in our parish affairs at the moment – and I hope to display these qualities once again at the PCC and provide a much-needed 'moral dimension' to St Albion's life.

Yours faithfully,
David Blunkett,
The Very Large House
With The Drive,
Posh St, St Albion's.

(The Editor reserves the right to print in full any letters that make the Vicar look like a decent bloke. A.C.)

Mr Prescott – A Clarification

I want first of all to refute any inferences that whilst on Parish business I was staying in a poncy hotel in the South of France of the type the vicar likes to swan about in!

I did not stay nor was I ever going to stay in the Hotel Resplendente on the Cote d'Amour as was inaccurately reportaged in various St Albion's publications, ie the Clarion, the Mercury, the Advertiser and other rags.

The nub of the fact is that I stayed in a modest, five-star establishment called the Hotel Excelsior, tucked away on the front, which is patronised only by honest, working folk from Saudi Arabia, Switzerland and California. So apologies are in order with regard to this one from everyone concerned.

And whilst on the subject of apologies, may I secondly make it clear that I never said that the travelling folk could come and camp in your back garden if they felt like it. The records will prove that this remark was taken out of context and what I *really* was suggesting was that there is plenty of space in the Millennium Tent for as many of our roaming friends as would wish to make it their home. Understood? Thank you.

J. Prescott,
The Working Men's Club, Nice.

Thought For The Week

The Vicar has chosen a special text:

"The first shall be last and the last first and the race shall not go to the swift nor the battle to the strong and I didn't lose last week just because the others won in fact I won because I was right all along"
(Book of Judges, Lords and Traitors, 12.4)

ST ALBION PARISH NEWS

2nd April 2005

Hullo!

And I'm sure you were all pleased with the fine weather I brought you over Easter!

Not that I'm claiming to have supernatural powers!

But come on! When your vicar prays for nice sunny weather and then, lo and behold, we have the hottest day of the year – well, you don't have to be a rocket scientist to see that two and two make four, do you? (Note to our treasurer Mr Brown – two and two do still make four, not minus £35 billion as some people around this parish seem to think!)

Anyway I wanted this week, firstly, to congratulate our new curate Mr Milburn on the marvellous job he's been doing, communicating our 'mission statement' to everyone in the parish!

Of course some people have been running Mr Milburn down behind his back, as they sit in the Britannia Arms sipping their 'Newcastle Brown' ales and indulging in negative backstabbing!

They even say that Mr Milburn hasn't got any 'big ideas'!

Well, hullo, how big an idea do you want?

How about these for starters:

- Better quality soap in St Albion's Cottage Hospital.
- Gypsies to be moved on from the churchyard.
- Our local Neighbourhood Watch to increase surveillance on the bus shelter between 6pm and 9pm.

AND (and it's a pretty big AND!) what about the biggest big idea of them all?

What I mean of course is that Number One Topic that we have been focusing on for the past day – namely SCHOOL DINNERS!!!

Yes, when it comes to big ideas, you can't get much bigger than that.

I think I can hear one of the Sunday School saying that it wasn't exactly my idea!

It was something that famous chef Jamie Oliver was going on about on the telly!

But what is it that the Good Book says? "Great minds think alike" (*Proverbs 9.10*).

I have never met Mr Oliver, though of course we've all seen him on the screen (and I have long looked on him as a good friend)!

But I'm glad that his views on the importance of school dinners have come to resemble my own so closely!

No, I think we all now realise that feeding young children with the right food is just as important as feeding their minds with the right ideas.

Left to themselves, I'm afraid children would eat chips and vote Conservative!

Which brings me to my seventh and final point this Christmas morning, which is that I have never felt fitter and better equipped to renew my calling to serve you all to the best of my ability – which, I would humbly suggest, is rather greater than that of the various other people who at the moment are going around suggesting that they could do better (namely, those who still think that two and two somehow makes minus £35 billion!).

No offence, Gordon, but like everything else about you, it doesn't quite add up!

Yours,

Tony

KIDZ CORNER

Nursery Rhymes Revisited
With the Vicar

♪ ♪

There's a hole in my budget,
Dear Tony, dear Tony.
There's a hole in my budget
Dear Tony, a hole.

Then fix it, dear Gordy, (x3)
Or you'll get the sack.

Hope you enjoy singing this one, kids!

St Albion's Primary School

Mrs Kelly has asked me to tell everyone that we should no longer use the derogatory and sexist phrase 'dinner ladies'. From now the helpers at our primary school should be known as "Catering Solution co-ordinators". T.B.

The Seven Deadly Sins

No.8 Apathy

There is no sin more deadly than apathy, from the Greek *apatheos* meaning a pathetic failure to go out and vote for the vicar in the parish elections.

It's all too easy to think that one person's vote doesn't make any difference, and that it's much easier just to stay at home and watch Dr Who on the television.

Well, we should remember that that was what happened to those "foolish virgins" in the Bible, when they could have been out casting their vote for the party that promised to bring down the price of oil in the supermarket.

And look what happened to them? They all fell over a cliff in the dark, because they didn't have any oil in their lamps to see by!

There's a lesson there for all of us, isn't there? I'm going to think about it while I lie down for a while! T.B.

PCC Elections

With Easter behind us, the next big date on the calendar is May 5th. So, can I make a special request to all those people who will insist on trying to bring religion into church affairs? Don't!

Surely they must have heard the old expression "Religion and religion don't mix"?

That's not to say that religion doesn't have its place – anyone who knows the difference between right and wrong will be voting for me – obviously – but we don't want to make a big deal about it in public. We're not like our American friends, such as Reverend Dubya, who is confident in the knowledge that he is doing the Lord's work – just like me.

Rev. Tonya Blair

The vicar would like to thank everyone who sent him Easter eggs...
As seen by local artist Mr de la Nougerede

ST ALBION PARISH NEWS

15th April 2005

LET THE PEOPLE DECIDE!!!

A personal message to every parishioner from your Vicar

This is the most important month in the whole history of St Albion. And the most important people in St Albion's are **you**, the congregation, the ordinary, down-to-earth, stupid people who come up to me in the street and shout rude things at me *(I really don't think we should put this bit in, Tony. A.Campbell, acting editor).*

Week after week for the last eight years, you've been listening to me preaching about what I think!

Now it's your turn to tell me what **you** think! Because you're the boss, and what a heavy responsibility that is!

It's **my** job over the next few weeks to listen very carefully to what you have to say on all the big issues of the day, and then to explain to you why you are wrong!

That makes sense, doesn't it! So let's look at some of my so-called 'faults', shall we?

Apparently some of you have been saying that I smile too much! Well, puh-lease!!

Since when has it been a sin to smile, for heaven's sake? Especially when you've got so many reasons to smile! Let's check 'em out, shall we?

Waiting lists at our college hospital – DOWN!

ASBOs on teenage yobs at the bus shelter – UP!

Number of chips served at St Albion's Primary School dinners – DOWN!

Number of apples served – UP!

Number of foxes killed by St Albion Vale foxhounds – THE SAME!

I could go on, but I'm too busy smiling!

I've even written a special chorus for us all to sing at next week's Evensong:

When you're smiling, when you're smiling,
The whole world votes for you
(repeat five times)

Words and music T. Blair 2005

Of course I am not going to tell **you** how to vote when the great moment comes for **you** to decide on the future of the parish.

It is entirely a matter between **you** and your conscience!

If you wish to see our beloved church in ruins, with vampires flitting through the burnt-out ashes of the nave, then of course you are perfectly entitled to support our local solicitor Mr Howard!

Alternatively, you may feel that our parish affairs would be better handled by someone with a serious drink problem – like Mr Kennedy from the United Reformed Liberal Democratic Church!

As I said at the beginning, it's entirely up to you! It's your choice. It's your vote and it will be your fault if you are stupid enough not to give your support to the most successful vicar St Albion's has ever had!

Yours in humility, Tony

Thought For The Week

"Hail Thee Festival Day!"

I am sure you will all have noticed that May 5 is Ascension Day, to commemorate the moment when Our Lord was finally taken up into heaven! Worth thinking about! T.B.

CONGRATULATIONS!

I know you would all like me to pass on your congratulations to Mr Birt on his forthcoming divorce. As you know, Mr Birt works in a little office in the vicarage attic and is responsible for all those pie charts you see at the back of the church by Mrs Jowell's roulette wheel – please *do* take the time to look at them. Mr Birt has put a lot of work into them and has expressed his disappointment at the lack of interest shown by parishioners.

Can I especially ask the children not to fire their bee-bee guns into the Venn diagram about reorganising the flower roster? It is not a target! Well, it is actually – but not that sort!

Tony Blair

Mr Prescott writes:

This is a note to informalise you about the new arrangingments for the forthcoming parish elections. Unlike in previous elections, you will no longer have to walk through the cold and pouring rain to the primary school and/or stop watching your favourite TV soap 'Desperate Vicars' Wives'!

This time, you don't even have to fill in the voting paper. Just send it to me in the post and our team of trained helpers, Mr Shifti and Mr Khruq, will do it all for you! Just send your voting paper to me: J. Prescott, The Working Men's Club, St Albion's, and in due course it will be submitted to our returning officer in full accordance with the law! J.P.

The Vicar's Team

No. 1
Mr Brown

I would like to introduce you to my closest and dearest colleague, Mr Brown.

As I have so often said in this newsletter before, Gordon has been a real rock in the past eight years, giving me his unqualified support 24/7. I cannot think of anyone who has contributed so much to my success! We all owe him a tremendous debt, namely £35 billion! T.B.

— Vale —

I am sure you would all wish to join me in regretting the passing of our former vicar, the Rev. J. Callaghan (1976-9). Older parishioners will have vivid memories of his brief time in charge of the parish, when rubbish piled up in the streets, corpses lay for weeks unburied in the churchyard and giant rats roamed freely through the parish, devouring toddlers as they were sent home from schools closed by striking miners! How different things are today, as the Rev. Callaghan was first to admit! On his deathbed he told me, with his much-loved and familiar smile, "Tony, I made a real mess of it. Thank the Lord you have come along to put it all right again. I hope they have the good sense to keep you on as vicar for ever". And with that he breathed his last and was gone! He was a very great man, although he wasn't any good! T.B.

ST ALBION PARISH NEWS

29th April 2005

An Important Announcement From The Editor, Mr Campbell

The Vicar has asked me to explain why this week there will be no parish newsletter.

This is because during the PCC elections it would be improper for the newsletter to appear, as this might influence parishioners into supporting the Vicar, which they will obviously be doing anyway, rather than voting for a vampire or a drunk. A.C.

ST ALBION PARISH NEWS

13th May 2005

THOUGHT FOR THE WEEK

"He that is first shall be first.
He that is last is nowhere!"

(Book of Polls, 13.7)

Hullo,

And, let's be honest, it's a humble "hullo" this morning and I won't pretend that you haven't given me a lot to think about during the course of our parish elections. There have been lessons to learn and messages to take on board. And many of you had some really interesting things to say, you know, about the great crusade against the Evil One, and all of that. And, hey, I respect your views!

In the days to come I shall certainly be mulling all these things over and coming up with some suggestions as to how we can reconcile our differences and move forward with a common agenda to the sort of future we can all agree about.

Because that's what you're telling me, isn't it? You're telling me that you believe that I'm the right guy for the job and that you trust me to deliver when the going gets tough. Because when you put your cross (symbolic or what?) next to the vicar's

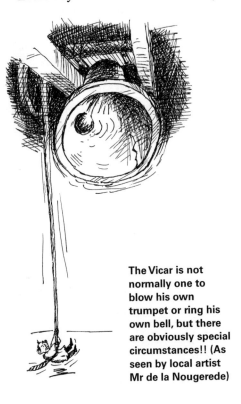

The Vicar is not normally one to blow his own trumpet or ring his own bell, but there are obviously special circumstances!! (As seen by local artist Mr de la Nougerede)

name you made it clear that you wanted *me* in the parish hot-seat and no one else!

Is that clear enough for everyone – not to mention any names, Gordon!

Yet, to hear some people talking, you might think that I had lost and that I was no longer vicar! Isn't that incredible?

The truth is that I have made history in the parish by being vicar three times in a row!!

That is the "Good News" that we want to shout from the rooftops. That is the "Good News" that we want to tell to the whole world! That is the "Good News" that the bells need to ring out!

And did anyone notice what day it was when I gained my great victory over the powers of darkness? Any of the children? No, Wayne, it wasn't the Champions League Semi-Final, though that was a great game, wasn't it, and you'll notice that the men in *red* won!

Yes, Rashid, *your* hand is up. That's right! Ascension Day! And how does that great hymn go that we sing on that great occasion? "Hail the day that sees him rise!" See any similarities there?

So that's the thought that I want you all to take home today. Your Vicar has listened to what you have to say – I have opened your letters, I have read your emails and your texts. And what I say to you is that I will treat your views with exactly the same degree of attention that I have always done in the past. And I can't say fairer than that, can I?

In fact, I've written a new chorus which we will all sing together at the great service of humble thanksgiving.

I'm listening and I'm learning.
But are you?
I'm listening and I'm learning.
Yes, it's true.
I'm listening and I'm learning.
But the Vicar's not for turning.
I'm listening and I'm learning.
Indeedy-do. (Repeat)

Words and music © T. Blair 2005.

Yours in victorious humility,

Tony

THANKS!

I'd like to give a big thank-you to all those who worked so long and hard to make our campaign such a success. You all did a splendid job and it would be invidious for me to single out one individual for special mention.

So sorry Gordon – there isn't room to thank you personally. T.B.

VALE

I'm sorry to have to say that our trusted curate, Mr Milburn, who disappeared during the election, has sadly decided to take early retirement in order to spend more time with his family – again. Goodness knows what they think about this! Perhaps they wish he'd spend more time with *us* and were glad to see the back of him. I know exactly how they feel – no offence, Alan!

So, thank you, Alan, for all you did – even though it wasn't very good or very helpful. T.B.

The Vicar's New Team Ministry

OLD	NEW
The Vicar	The Vicar
Mr Prescott	Mr Brown
Mr Brown	Mr Prescott
Mr Blunkett	Mr Straw
Mr Straw	Mr Blunkett
Mrs Jowell	Mrs Hewitt
Mr Reid	Mr Hoon
Mr Hoon	Mr Reid
Mrs Hewitt	Mrs Jowell

Yes, it's all change at St Albion's. Remember – Forward Not Backwards! T.B.

A Safe Pair of Hands!

Mr Blunkett leads the congregation in prayers of thanksgiving for keeping his house and getting his job back. Well done, David!

To Remember In Your Prayers

● Mr Galloway, who suggested that I would burn in hell. May he remember that people who insult the Vicar are much more likely to burn in hell or be struck by lightning – particularly when they have been sucking up to the Islamic community, and let us pray that none of the more extreme members of that community may take offence at Mr Galloway's remarks and decide to chop his hands off! T.B.

ST ALBION PARISH NEWS

27th May 2005

Hullo,

And today I want to focus on two little words both beginning with the same two little letters 'R' and 'E'.

Can any of the children guess what the words are? Yes, Sonali? 'Resign'. No, that's not one of them. Omid? 'Retire'. No that's not one of them either, and it's not funny actually so the rest of you can stop smirking.

No the words I am thinking of are 'Respect' and 'Reform'. Let's just consider those two words shall we?

What do we mean when we say we 'respect' someone? We mean that we are polite to them because we know that they are doing their job and we are not going to criticise them even if they make mistakes – which they don't anyway!

But most of all 'respecting' someone means accepting that they know better than we do and that it would be wrong of us to want them to give up their job and possibly hand over to someone else who isn't as good as them and might even be a disaster!

That's 'Respect', OK?

Which brings me to the second of those two very important little words that I want you all to be thinking about as we go forward into this new chapter in the life of St Albion's.

And, hey, they might be little words but they're mighty big concepts! (And that's from the Greek 'con-ceptos' meaning an idea stolen from conservatives.)

'Reform'. What do we mean by 'reform'? It certainly doesn't mean that what came before was bad – unless of course we go all the way back to 1997! No, obviously, a lot of what's been going on in recent years has been very good!

It's just that it's our job now to make it even better!

And that's why I've asked Mr Birt to draw up some 'blue-sky' plans for some much needed reforms to carry us into a wholly new era!

His first strategy is what he calls the 'Parish Energising and New Ideas Solution' (or PENIS, for short).

This is very exciting and I want everyone to grab hold of Mr Birt's PENIS plan and embrace it with both hands!

So those are the words I want you all to take away with you – Respect, Reform and PENIS.

Which brings me to my fifth and final point.

A lot of parishioners I know have been saying that I was wrong to ask Mr Blunkett back onto the PCC, just because he has gone mad.

Well, all I can say is that David has been through a very difficult period in his life and I really do think we all of us now owe it, both to David and to ourselves, to show compassion and to help him to rebuild his confidence as he begins to sort out the unfortunate mess that someone who shall be nameless (Gordon!) has made of the parish pension fund!

But I'm glad to say that a very good start has already been made on this. Your vicar's pension has been secured and 'ring-fenced' at £3 million a year.

So that, when I eventually decide to hang up my dog-collar, at least I shan't be having to sleep in one of those cardboard boxes in the churchyard.

You see. 'Reform' of our pension plan, and 'Respect' for the vicar. It's those two 'R's' in action.

In fact, I've written a special chorus which we're all going to sing at next week's One Parent Family Service (including our new Sunday Club for the Under-5's)!

Reform, reform.
It's got to be the norm.
Respect, respect.
It's what we all expect. (Repeat)

© Words and music T. Blair 2005

Yours respectfully (!),

Tony

P.S. The acronym PENIS has led to some giggling in the back pews by our more adolescent parishioners so we have deemed it advisable to revert to our first thoughts on the Parish Research Investigation Committee for Knowledge – or PRICK for short.

SODUTOO *with Mr Brown*

Last week, readers were given a blank grid and asked to fill in the missing numbers, so that the parish books would balance.
   No one got exactly the right answer, I'm afraid, but it was:

£	3	7	0	0	0	0	0	0	0	0	0

G.B.

Women's Groups

*T*he Vicar's wife, Mrs Booth, gave a very interesting talk on how to increase the power of women in the parish. The solution to this problem, she said, was very simple. In future, only women should be allowed to stand for the PCC. We all wondered why we hadn't thought of it ourselves!

Mrs Jowell gave a vote of thanks, and suggested that the next vicar should be a woman. Who better, she asked, than Mrs Booth herself?

Refreshments, made by Mrs Hewitt, included 'gingerbread men' which everyone enjoyed biting the heads off and then throwing the rest in the bin!

A Wind of Change!

I know that many of you will be delighted to see the new-look spire of the church which is now a giant wind turbine providing enough electricity to boil the entire kettle of water needed for the after service coffee!

Isn't that great! The windmill was erected by Mr Doughty's excellent company "Wind Farms Я Us" who were awarded the contract purely on the grounds of merit – and not because, as some mean-spirited parishioners are claiming, he made a large donation to parish funds – shame on you, you cynics!

If anyone is in-spired (get it?) by our example they can purchase their own private wind farm from Mr Doughty's website www.indfarm.co.uk.

 ## St Albion's Primary School
Salve!

Mr Adonis, who joins us as a new school governor. Although he is only 18, Mr Adonis has some brilliant new ideas, such as selling the school to a group of local businessmen. They are hoping to rename it as the Kwikfit Academy ("We fit you for the world of work, and quick!"). Great to have you on board, Andrew!

KIDDIES CORNER
with Miss Blears

For this week's competition, children are invited to colour in a picture of a typical hooligan who has been causing trouble in the parish. Just imagine that he should be made to wear a really nastyish orange uniform, so that everyone will know he is Charles Kennedy!

PS. His face should be red.
Can you guess why?
Signed,
Auntie Hazel

ST ALBION PARISH NEWS

10th June 2005

Hullo,

And you remember that last week I talked about two very important word beginning with the letters 'R' and 'E'.

They were 'Respect' and 'Refrain'.

Well this week I've got another one, and, no, Rashid, it's still not 'Resign', and that joke is still not funny and clever and it's wearing very thin. Like my patience with Mr Geldof! But more of that later.

No, the word I have in mind this week is 'Reflection'. It's what you see when you look in the mirror, unless of course you're Mr Howard (when you wouldn't see anything, because he's a vampire!).

"A time for reflection." That's something we're all very much in need of these days!

People are always coming up to me and asking "Vicar, what are you going to do?" about such and such a thing.

And the answer is "I'm not going to do anything. I'm simply going to reflect" on whatever it is.

That's what's important, when things don't turn out quite as you expected (not that they don't, but it's just that sometimes they do!).

This week, as you've all probably gathered, we've experienced a little bit of 'turbulence' over our very important Oecumenical Union project along with all our brothers and sisters in other countries across Europe.

It seems that some of the congregations in France and Holland are not entirely happy with the way we've been running things!

And once again I hear the cry going up "Vicar, this is terrible. It's all coming apart. You've got to do something!".

Well my answer is "Hey, I am doing something! I am reflecting. I am taking stock. I an thinking very hard about the way ahead. I am asking that very difficult question which we all of us have to face at one time or another in our lives, which is "I know I am right, but why can't all these silly people agree with me?".

So to anyone who wants to come up to me in Tesco, or anywhere else, and say, "Vicar, it's all gone pear-shaped – why don't you admit it?", my reply will be to push them into the fresh fruit counter and say "look who's pear-shaped now!".

For all those who might be feeling suicidal or depressed about the so-called failure of our oecumenical project, I would merely ask them to 'reflect' on the wise words of that holy man Jack (or St Raw as he was known) in his letter to The Guardian, "There is no such thing as a disaster. It is merely an opportunity waiting to happen".

Isn't that something worth spending time 'reflecting' on?

And talking of reflection, something our talkative friend Mr Geldof might consider 'reflecting' on, as he goes around telling everyone that we've got to 'save Africa', is the fact that someone has already decided to save Africa, and it's not Mr Geldof!

No, Rashid, it's not Mr Brown either, and if you're going to carry on being silly, I'm going to have to exclude you from our Sunday club!

No, the person who has been going on about the need to save Africa long before Mr Geldof had even heard of it was your own vicar!

And when it comes to playing the guitar and writing songs, I think you'll find that I am probably ahead of our Irish friend there too!

In fact, I have written a brand-new chorus for this week's Evensong entitled 'Save the World':

Don't they know it's Christmas
Now that I am here,
Africa can live again
Without hate or fear.
Save the world, save the world.
(repeat)

Words and music T. Blair.

Yours,

Tony

The Vicar takes time out for "reflection" – as seen by local artist Mr de la Nougerede

Letter From the Former Churchwarden, Mr Mandelson

Dear Sir,

In the light of the sad news from the European Outreach Programme, now would scarcely be the right time for the Vicar to even think of stepping down.

If there is one person with the experience, knowledge, wisdom and humanity to guide the European Mission through the choppy waters that lie ahead, it is the Reverend Anthony Blair, M.A. Oxon.

To think of a lesser person, possibly Scottish, possibly rather shabbily dressed and possibly with a dour, hangdog expression unlikely to appeal to anybody let alone the cosmopolitan modern European ministers of the Continent, would be folly.

No, the vicar must remain for at least the next ten years and possibly longer with the assistance of his faithful and able servants.

Yours faithfully and ably,

P. Mandelson,
The European Outreach Mission,
Rue des Matelots,
Bruxelles.

 A LETTER FROM THE OFFICE OF MS CHERIE BOOTH Q.C.

Dear Sir,

It has come to my notice that a number of your parishioners have been making allegations to the effect that I am seeking to take pecuniary advantage of my position as the wife of your vicar. This innuendo has apparently been inspired by the fact that I am shortly to give a lecture in Washington. It is only by the purest chance that my lecture happens to coincide with a long-arranged visit by my husband to his friend the Rev. Dubya of the Church of the Latter-Day Morons, along with Sister Condy, Brother Rumsfield and other high ranking Morons. The fact that my talk is called 'How to Make Money Out of Being the Vicar's Wife' has no bearing whatever on these unfounded and slanderous allegations, and I hereby warn any parishioner who is party to repeating them that I shall not hesitate to issue a writ of scandalum magnatum to be brought before the supreme court of the land, namely my friend Mr Falconer. You have been warned!

Yours faithfully,
Cherie Booth, Q.C.

ST ALBION PARISH NEWS

24th June 2005

Hullo!

And, as you can imagine, my message to all my parishioners this week is 'stand firm'!

In the words of perhaps the greatest incumbent St Albion's ever had before 1997, "The Vicar's not for turning!".

I am referring, of course, to my problems with our French friend Monsignor Chirac, who this time has gone several steps too far!

At our recent Oecumenical Union Council in Belgium, this so-called man of the cloth had the audacity to demand that I paid for everyone's lunch out of St Albion's Parish funds!

Talk about outrageous! To begin with, I didn't have a starter and I only drank tap water throughout the meal.

Whereas Pastor Schroeder ordered a huge pile of bratwurst and sauerkraut, and Monsignor Chirac himself insisted on tucking into platesful of pâté de foie gras, snails and frogs' legs, washed down with bottle after bottle of expensive French wine!

Hey, don't get me wrong! People can eat and drink what they like! And these are my friends and colleagues!

So I have no objection to us all having a jolly good meal together every so often – and if they want to overdo it a bit, that's their problem!

But, look, they can't then sit around when the bill arrives and expect all the hard-working parishioners of St Albion's to dig deep into their pockets and pay for their food mountains and wine lakes!

So I said to them, in my best French, "Non!". I told them in no uncertain manner that there was absolutely no question whatsoever of me agreeing to pay a penny (or euro-cent!) more than was fair!

I don't want to be petty, but Monsignor Chirac's share of the bill alone was 938 euros, ie fourteen times more than mine!

Is that fair, I ask? "Non!" again is the answer!

So, you can see, I really did take a firm line on this and I wasn't going to give a single inch (or millimetre, as we now call it).

Don't get me wrong. When I say firm, I don't mean I'm not prepared to negotiate.

That would be silly, to say that one's not prepared to talk about something at all, and not come to a sensible agreement.

In the words of our good friend, Mr Mandelson, who has been

running our outreach programme in Brussels for the last few months, "Just because you say 'non', that doesn't stop you meaning 'oui'!".

So, in the end, after many hours of discussion, which I don't mind admitting got at times pretty heated, I did agree to pay the bill! But I asked the others to pay me back, which they promised to consider very seriously and would let me know their decision in the next few years.

I think you'll agree that this was, in the circumstances, a sensible compromise and, in many ways, a victory for my policy of being absolutely firm!

Yours,

Tony

A LETTER FROM THE OFFICE OF MS CHERIE BOOTH Q.C.

Dear Sir,

I must remind your readers that when I am invited to give a lecture in Malaysia on the important topic of "What It Is Like To Be Married To The Vicar", I am only doing so in my private capacity as a professional lawyer and as a world-acknowledged expert on human rights. And one of my human rights, I would remind parishioners, is to make as much money as possible out of being married to the Vicar. So, if I choose to open the Sleeping Tiger Shopping Mall in Kuala Lumpur, at the invitation of that highly-respected local businessman Mr Del Boi, that is entirely a matter between me and my accountants. Anyone who suggests otherwise will lay themselves open to a writ of scandalum magnatum and risks a sum in damages of not less than the 700 million Malaysian Kokh (£30,000) which I am to receive for my talk.

Yours faithfully,
C. Booth, Q.C.

A Notice From Mrs Kelly, the new Chair of the Governors, St Albion's Primary School (shortly to be renamed the Kwikfit Beacon Academy)

Hullo, working mums and working dads!

I've got great news. As from this autumn, you never need worry again about rushing back from work to pick up your kids from school! Here's why – the school is going to be open 24 hours a day! There's going to be a Breakfast Club, A Lunch Club, An Afternoon Club, A Night Club and a Sleepover Club. So you can drop your kids off at school and pick them up months later, if you feel like it! We've all been worried about the effects of poor parenting on today's kids. And this is a brilliant solution. They need never see you again!

Mrs Kelly

Says the Vicar: *Hey, can I interrupt here?! This is a great idea, Ruth. And it's so great that I've written a special chorus for next week's evensong:*

*On Mother Kelly's doorstep
You can dump your kids all day,
For only 50 quid a week
They can work and sleep and play,
On Mother Kelly's doorstep
Down St Albion's way.*

© *Words and music T. Blair.*

**The Vicar's wife campaigns
for "Fee Speech"!
As seen by local artist
Mr de la Nougerede**

ST ALBION PARISH NEWS

8th July 2005

Due to popular demand, we are reprinting the Vicar's sermon to the Sunday Club in full

Hullo, kids!

Now, can any of you tell me what great event we are celebrating this year? No, not Live8, Rashid, though that is jolly important and I'll be talking about that later. No, something that happened all of two hundred years ago – even before I became the vicar here... No one knows?

That's a pity, especially since standards are so high in our parish schools at the moment, thanks to Mrs Kelly. Well, I'll tell you. It was the Battle of Trafalgar. No, nothing to do with the Poll Tax riots... though a good try!

Look, here's the story. There was once a very bad Frenchman called Napoleon. He thought himself so clever and so powerful that he could take over all the countries in Europe – Germany, France, Italy, Spain and even Britain!

No one was brave enough to stand up to him. They all ran away as soon as the big bully came into sight.

But there was one person who had the guts to take him on. A young, handsome, brave Englishman (not a Scotsman, you notice!).

And this hero was called Horatio Nelson and he said to Napoleon Chirac, "No. England expects every man not to pay any duty". No wonder this great man, Tony Nelson, has gone down in history as the greatest Englishman who ever lived. And all because he was brave enough to defeat the French in the famous Battle of

The Winner Of The Children's Competition – To Draw A Picture Of The Vicar *(surely Lord Nelson?)*

Adelaide de la Nougerede (Aged 7)

the Rebate all those years ago.

Well, that's enough of a history lesson – and something else I'm going to make history **is** poverty.

I expect you've all seen Saint Bob Geldof on the television preaching his message to his followers. Good for Bob, I say! But let's not forget who it was who first drew the world's attention to the problems of Africa! No, not Bono, Rageh, and certainly not Mr Brown, thank you, Shane. The person who actually started the whole ball rolling was your vicar when he announced that he would "heal the scars of Africa". What a moving picture that paints, and doesn't it give us all something to think about while Mr Geldof is playing his guitar?

Now some of you might ask me, "Vicar, you're going to save Europe. You're going to save Africa. What else can you do?".

Well, I'm not one to blow my own trumpet, but, as the Good Book tells us, "There is no point in hiding your light under a George Bush". So, I might as well tell you that next up, I will be saving the world from pollution!

Isn't that quite a tall order? you say. Well, not for a five-times-a-night man!! Sorry, kids, you'll have to ask your mum and dad what that means when you're a little bit older!!! Except for you obviously, Coleen, because you're pregnant.

Anyway the point is, "If you want something done, you ask a busy man" *(Book of Cliches, 7.3)*.

And, hey, I'm probably the busiest man in the world. Yet people keep coming up to me in Tesco's and saying, "Vicar, when are you going to retire?".

Goodness me, what a silly question!! As Brother Rumsfeld said about Iraq only the other day, "We're going to finish the job if it takes two years, five years, ten years or a hundred years".

What a message of hope that is from one of America's leading Morons.

Is it just me or is it hot in here? I think I might have to go and lie down for a bit. Who said "It'll make a change from lying standing up?" Come on, own up! Someone said it. I bet it was you, Rashid. Right, you can't come on the Cubs outing to Warminster-on-Sea. That'll teach you. You see, zero tolerance.

I dunno... kids today. They think they can do whatever they like. That Mrs Kelly has got a lot to answer for...

(The Vicar was helped out of the pulpit at this point, suffering from an acute case of heatstroke and was sadly unable to finish his sermon.)

A CORRECTION
FROM THE OFFICE OF
MS CHERIE BOOTH Q.C.

In the last issue of the newsletter, I may have given the impression that I was going to open the Sleeping Tiger Shopping Mall in Kuala Lumpur, at the invitation of the respected local businessman Mr Del Boi.

This is, of course, quite untrue. I never had any intention of opening the shopping mall in question nor of accepting any free gifts that Mr Boi might choose to send round in a large lorry to my hotel room.

Anyone who tries to suggest to the contrary will receive a writ of Harum Scarum from the offices of my friend Mr Falconer and will have to pay damages equivalent to the value of the goods in the lorry.

Yours threateningly,
C. Booth Q.C.

MR BIRT'S 'BLUE SKY' REPORTS

Mr Birt has been working on behalf of the Vicar on a number of very important issues for the last five years. I have now decided to print these up and place them at the back of the church.

Some of you might find them worth looking at, but frankly I wouldn't bother. For example Mr Birt has concluded that crime is caused by criminals, drug addicts take a lot of drugs, people who are ill need the Health Service, transport is required for people who want to travel and that children need education to learn things.

Interesting though these findings are, we shall not be requiring Mr Birt's services for too much longer and his room in the attic may well be given to Mr Blunkett as an extra office. We all look forward to Mr Birt's new reports on whether the Pope is Catholic and whether bears defecate in the woods!! (Thanks to Mr Prescott for the joke, although in his typical bluff way John didn't use the word 'defecate'!! T.B.)

A Message From The Rev. Dubya Bush Of The Church Of The Latter-Day Morons

Brothers and Sisters in Great Englandland!

The crusade goes on despite some reversalities and difficultitudes – but are we a Brotherhood of Quitters? No, no, Siree! And are we grateful to your pastor, the Reverend Tiny Bloom for his steadfast loyalty and supportivity in the fight against the evil one – Yea, verily yea!!

In return I would like to say to Pastor Bloom, do not expect any favours in return, Buddy! Particularly over the minor matters of the imminent destruction of the globe by fire and brimstone-style warming!

For as it is written in the Good Book "If a neighbour offers you his coat, take it and run away".

So thanks Tiny for everything, but when it comes to this long-hair hippy nonsense about the sun fryin' up the planet like a barbecue – I say "Hogwash"! Tell it to the marines – that's if there are any of them left alive!

Yours in the Lord,
Rev. Dubya

Congratulations

👍 To EUAN BLAIR, who has won a special scholarship to travel to America as an intern for Rev. Dubya's Church of the Latter-Day Morons. Euan will be doing top-level research for the Morons. Very few young men get such an opportunity on the basis of their own merits and it is a tribute to Euan that he was chosen out of hundreds of candidates to win this prestigious academic scholarship: The Rev. Dubya Open Award For Sons Of My Friends. As Euan put it, "I'm following in my Dad's footsteps, I'm working for Duyba!" T.B.

ST ALBION PARISH NEWS

22nd July 2005

7/7

Hullo!

And let me begin by saying how deeply touched I have been by
the messages which have been flooding into the vicarage from all
over the world, thanking me simply for being here.

At moments of great crisis, people instinctively turn to someone
they know they can trust. Someone who will find the right words
for the occasion. Someone who will be able to put on the right sort
of sad face, as I was able to do on a former occasion, after the
death of our beloved 'People's Princess'.

Can I just quote from some of the very moving tributes which I
have received in recent days from all manner of parishioners, even
those who in the past have criticised me for no good reason.

"Dear Vicar," starts one from a local solicitor, a Mr Howard, "In
times of crisis, such as this, we look for a certain type of moral
leadership. Someone who is capable of rising to the occasion and
displaying the supreme qualities of vicarmanship, as you did in that
unforgettable sermon where you told us all that it was 'a very sad
day' and that it wasn't your fault."

There were hundreds, if not thousands, of similar messages.
Letters, texts, emails, even floral tributes placed along the railings
of the vicarage.

But there's always someone, isn't there, who wants to try and
spoil everything for everyone else.

In this case, I might have known that it would be our friend Mr
Galloway, who started heckling from the back of the church that if
it hadn't been for my support for the Rev. Dubya in his crusade
against the Evil One, then none of these sad events would have
happened.

Talk about bad taste! At a time when the whole community is
united in grief, how dare he start looking around for the cause of it?

Should he not show a modicum of respect for all those people
who are supporting their vicar, and who certainly don't want to be
listening to the lunatic ravings of some embittered Scotsman!

And, talking of embittered Scotsmen, I hope we have now heard
the last of all that talk about me retiring and handing the parish

over to someone else (Mr Brown might have some idea who I am talking about!).

If one thing has become certain in the past few weeks, it is that "all has now changed utterly, in the twinkling of an eye," as the Good Book has it.

And let's not be fooled by that old cliché about "no one being indispensable" that may be true most of the time, but there are occasions when someone proves to be exactly that!

After all, that word is from the Latin 'indispensibilis', meaning a person who, if he was to resign, would bring about the collapse of our entire Western civilisation!

Yours (in Dispensibly!),

Tony

The Vicar thinks he might still be around to hand out the prizes! As seen by local artist Mr de la Nougerede

A letter from Mr Blunkett's solicitors, Bindweed and Bindweed

Dear Sir,

Our attention has been drawn to a musical entertainment currently being produced by the St Albion Players entitled "Yes Sir, That's My Baby".

My client, Mr David Blunkett, formerly of the Neighbourhood Watch, takes grave exception to the above and gives notice that unless the play ceases forthwith he will take action under the recently passed Prevention of Plays About David Blunkett Act (2005).

Signed,

Geoffrey Blindman

A Word of Thanks

Once again we should record our heartfelt gratitude to Mr Mittal for giving £2 million to parish funds. Mr Mittal's solicitor has asked me to make it clear that were anyone to suggest that Mr Mittal is expecting anything whatever in return for his generous gift, then such a person would have to face the full rigour of the law. Mr Mittal's privacy is very important to him, which is why he has made this anonymous donation. He is so private that even Mr Mandelson does not know where he lives! (No offence, Peter, and thanks to Mr Bremner for this excellent joke!)

Of course, Lord Mittal is not looking for any personal preferment. His only motivation in making this very handsome donation was to express his sincere admiration for everything the Vicar has done for the parish, especially the business community, and even more especially the Anglo-Romanian Steel Trading Community. Anyone who suggests to the contrary may find themselves looking at a privacy suit for which the likely damages might well equate to a sum, shall we say, of around £2 million (or the number you first thought of). T.B.

Not True!!

The former editor of this newsletter has instructed us to publish the following statement on his behalf, in relation to his recent business trip to New Zealand to promote the tour made by the St Albion's Lions rugby football team.

*I am f****** sickened by some of the f****** garbage which certain scumbags in the local media have chosen to write about my part in the failure of our local rugby team to win a single game "down under". It has even been alleged on the St Albion's Hospital Radio that I know f*** all about f****** rugby! So f****** what I ask! I know a f*** of a lot about boxing, and all I can say is that if I ever meet any of these c**** again, I will smash their f****** faces in. The only things that will be "all black" will be their f****** eyes! Understood?*

Signed
Alastair Campbell,
Chief Communications and
Corporate Relations Director,
The St Albion's Lions World Tour
email al.camp@fujimmy.co.uk

ANNOUNCEMENTS

MR BYERS, who served on the PCC (Railway Sub-committee) some time ago, tells me, "I may have told a lie but it was a long time ago and I can't remember if I did or if I did why I did. So perhaps I didn't."

This shows that Mr Byers acted in good faith and there is no need for him to be punished. As the Good Book says, "Thou shalt not bear false witness except under very special circumstances" *(Book of Trains 7.15).*

Mr Byers prays for forgiveness

ST ALBION PARISH NEWS

5th August 2005

Hullo,

And I think we've all been very much reminded this week that we are all of us living in a very different world from the one we were living in last week!

A world in which the old certainties have been suddenly swept away. And, hey, there's nothing wrong with sweeping away old certainties!

That's what we do with ideas which have passed their sell-by date!

How can we get new certainties in this life unless we've had the courage to get rid of all those old certainties which are no longer relevant to the world we're living in! Which, as I've already said, is very different from the one we were all living in an hour ago!

So one thing I am certain about is that we've got to junk all that dated old nonsense about "civil liberties" and "habeas corpus" and "Magna Carta". Hey, who speaks Latin anymore? It's the 21st century isn't it, and…

…Excuse me, Tony, but I demand my basic human right to interrupt this newsletter in order to point out that most of what you have already said is utter nonsense and the very opposite of what people like us should stand for [*writes Cherie Booth QC in a personal capacity as a senior barrister-at-law and spokesperson for the human rights community*]. **What my husband has totally failed to grasp (along with such little matters as how to use the washing machine, the iron and the video!) is that, once you take away people's human rights, you become just as bad as the people who are trying to take away your life.**

As I said in my private speech to 3,000 lawyers in Malaysia (which I wish to emphasise I was only visiting in my private capacity as the Vicar's wife), if you are worried about your human rights, St Albion's is privileged to have some of the world's very top practitioners in this field.

It would be wrong for me, in my private capacity, to name names, but the company I work for is internationally regarded as the best human rights practise in the world employing the wife of your vicar (and our telephone number can be found in the book under "M"!).

For example, if you want your daughter to go to the local primary school in a burka and her headmistress complains, then you should contact us to sue the school for a flagrant infringement of your daughter's human rights, and to demand a sum of damages not exceeding the school's budget for several years.

You will then be able to buy your daughter all the burkas she wants!

…I'm sorry, Cherie, but I've just got to step in at this point, to remind you that this is the newsletter and I am actually the vicar…

…be quiet, Tony, I'm making a very important point, not just waffling on in a well-meaning but totally pointless way, just because you don't know what to say because your good friend the Rev. Dubya hasn't rung you up recently to give you one of his little pep talks about the need for one of his mad crusades against the Evil One!

…Cherie, honestly, this really isn't very good timing. I mean, you know, there's quite a lot going on, and some of us are playing our socks off to, you know, try to find something helpful to say…

…if you'll just let me finish, Tony, I was making the rather important point that there are a lot of people who need help in these uncertain times, and it's my job to give them that help.

For example, imagine that you are the headmistress of our local primary school and that one of the girls turns up in a burka, in flagrant breach of the school rules and the headmistress's basic human right to run her own school in the way she thinks best.

Obviously you want to sue the girl and her parents for every penny they've got! And that's where we come in…

…honestly, Cherie, I really don't think that this is appropriate at this particular time, and I must therefore ask you…

...oh, so a woman's not allowed to say anything now, is that it?

Perhaps you'd like me to wear a burka and walk four paces behind you as if we were still living in the middle ages!

I tell you, you'll be hearing from myself, and I warn you that I'll be sueing you for every penny we've got! Which, incidentally, due to the miserable salary they pay you for being vicar, i.e a pathetic £166,000 a year, is not very much. Which is why I have to go on private speaking tours to places like bloody Malaysia, to keep up our payments on the mortgage...

...that's really below the belt, Cherie...

...oh, so it's my fault now, is it? I see!

...I didn't say that, Cherie...

...I'm not going to argue with you, Tony. If you can't see how stupid and irrational you're being, then there's no point in my wasting my time. I'm leaving this newsletter right now.

...Well, I think that what that shows is that this is a parish where everyone is encouraged to speak their mind and they'll all be listened to, irrespective of whether they're talking complete nonsense or not!

And if even the Vicar's wife stands a very good chance of being placed under house arrest by armed officers in St Albion's Neighbourhood Watch operating their shoot-to-kill policy then so be it!

As I said, it's a very different world from the one we were living in when I started this newsletter ten minutes ago!

Yours,

Tony

ST ALBION PARISH NEWS

19th August 2005

Important notice

The Vicar and his family are currently enjoying a well-deserved break, but for security reasons we are unable to reveal in which part of the world they are spending their holiday. Nevertheless, we are grateful to Tony for giving up some of his valuable recreation time to pay his tribute to a much-loved and loyal colleague, our late organist Mr Cook.

The Vicar's Tribute

Hullo, and a very sad 'hullo' it is on this sad occasion. The word has just reached me of the sad passing of Mr Cook while he was on holiday in his native Scotland.

Our thoughts naturally go out to the two Mrs Cooks at this very sad time.

All of you, I am sure, will have your own memories of Robin. But I have more than most.

When I arrived in this parish I had no hesitation in appointing him to the supremely important post of our parish organist.

Here was a man supremely fitted for the job to which history had called him.

Blessed with a brilliant and agile brain, an impish sense of humour and a single-minded dedication to the task in front of him, he was also one of the finest public speakers our parish has ever known.

His witty and acerbic speeches at our annual harvest suppers were a delight which none of us will ever forget.

And above all Robin had an unshakeable sense of loyalty.

Or so I thought! But then, alas, the day came when I began to realise that Robin had his own agenda.

I'm sure you will all remember those dark days when the Rev. Dubya called us all to stand together in support of his great crusade to eliminate the Evil One from the world.

Never was it more important that the parish team should stick together and present a united front in the face of the threat that then confronted us.

But for reasons known only to Robin, he chose instead to break ranks and to make every effort to undermine the great cause on which we had embarked.

Far be it for me at this particularly sad time to rake up unhappy memories from the past, when we are all quite rightly recalling Robin's many sterling qualities, few though they may have been.

But I have to say that his conduct at that time and subsequently was the most unforgivable act of treachery I have known in my long career in the church!

It is perhaps idle to speculate as to what Robin's true motivation was in betraying me as he did at that time.

Many of you, I know, who heard him speak at various occasions at that time were of the opinion that poor Robin had experienced some kind of mental breakdown.

I would perhaps prefer a more charitable explanation.

It was no secret that Robin had a particular fondness for the drink associated with his native Scotland.

Again his visits to the betting shop bore sad testament to the addiction to gambling which sadly had him in its grip.

No wonder that his manner of speech became the object of ridicule. Attention was also inevitably drawn to his ridiculous beard and staring eyes!

For a long time I tried to overlook his manifest failings and to

THE VICAR MOURNS:
As seen by local artist
Mr de la Nougerede

turn a blind eye to his absurd and outrageous conduct.

But in the end I had to remember that there are few words in the English language bigger and more important than that seven-letter word 'Loyalty'.

And this was the word, it seemed, that Robin had forgotten the meaning of.

It was bad enough that he should have shown such a lack of loyalty to me as his vicar.

But, hey, I can take that! That's my job!

What I think none of us can forgive, or should, is Robin's heartless betrayal of his faithful and long-suffering wife Margaret.

When rumours first reached me of certain goings-on in the organ loft between Robin and the girl he got in to turn the pages of his music and to stay behind to collect up the hymn books, I tried to turn a deaf ear.

But in the end Robin's behaviour became so shameless that my patience gave way.

I knew that I had to get tough. So I asked Mr Campbell to ring him up and order him to get divorced at once, to prevent any further scandal in the parish.

I know a lot of you will be saying that I should have let bygones be bygones, and flown home to pay my last respects at Robin's funeral.

But I don't think you realise how inconvenient this would have been, not to mention the expense involved.

I am sure you appreciate that I and my family don't get many days off in the course of a hard-working year, and to expect me to break off from my well-earned holiday in honour of a man who, frankly, I held in the utmost contempt, would be ridiculous.

Even if I was still back at home in the vicarage, I knew that it would be hard to justify dropping important parish business to pay homage to a man who had not only stabbed me in the back but also abandoned his wife and family to run off with his secretary!

Yours ever,

Tony

P.S. Apologies to Mr Prescott, whom I know had been struggling to pen his usual August newsletter to you all while 'holding the fort' in my absence. But I am sure we will somehow find room for his effort next year (which will also give us time to correct any spelling mistakes!).

Parish Postbag

From Mr Blunkett, formerly in charge of our Neighbourhood Watch

Dear Sir,

I hereby give notice that in the Vicar's absence, at this time when we are all under attack from the 'enemies within', I have taken charge, as I am far more experienced in these matters than anyone else in the parish, particularly Mr Prescott who frankly does not know his

Yours faithfully,
D. Blunkett,
Grace and Favour House,
Posh Street.

(The Editor reserves the right to cut all letters for reasons of space. J.P.)

To Remember In Your Prayers

● Mr McCririck, whom I gather made a fool of himself at Mr Cook's funeral by being rude about me. Let us pray that this unfortunate self-publicist with his silly hats and ridiculous sideburns may gain a speedy exit from a world that obviously troubles him. May he be given the wisdom to see that those who chose not to attend the funeral were honouring Mr Cook just as much as those who drank too much and talked nonsense at the service! T.B.

KIDZ HOLIDAY QUIZ

Where's Tony? Can you guess where the vicar is on holiday? Just choose from these fun destinations and you could win a free trip round the vicarage with Mr Prescott!

Is it:

a) Skegness?

b) Bournemouth?

c) One of his rich friends' luxury villas on the island of Grand Fribi in the Caribbean?

Holiday Special
Visit the Vicarage!!!

In the Vicar's absence, ordinary parishioners can have the rare opportunity to visit the vicarage and to be given a personal guided tour by 'the man in charge', John Prescott.

Says one lucky holidaymaker, Mrs Patel: *"The family were just walking past the vicarage, hoping to catch a glimpse of the vicar sitting at his desk writing one of his sermons, when a stout gentleman rushed out and said, 'They're away, him and his missus. Why don't I show you round. He's left me the key!'.*

"Imagine our surprise when only minutes later we were given a privileged glimpse of the room in which the vicar does it five times a night!"

Opening hours: Weekdays 9-5. Closed weekends.
Coach parties catered for by arrangement.

THE LISTENING PARISH

Are you a member of an ethnic minority? Then come and meet the PCC's new Inclusivity Co-ordinator Hazel Blears. Next week she will be out and about in the Parish, seeking the views of anyone who may be suffering from identity crisis as to how they would like to be classified – e.g. Eskimo-Irish, Bangladeshi-Jewish, Chinese-American-Indian etc.

Hazel will be at these venues next week:

Wed. 10 - 11.
Safekwik Supermarket, Falconer Drive.
Thurs. 10 - 11.
Hislop's Sports Boutique, Staplehurst Road.
Fri. 10 - 11.
'Poor Pussy' Veterinary Clinic, Wapshott Avenue.
Sat. 10 - 11.
DVD Centre (formerly the public library) Milburn Lane.

Or log on to www.hazelshereforyou.blog.spot.com

ST ALBION PARISH NEWS

2nd September 2005

Hullo!

And congratulations to all the children who guessed the right answer to the quiz question "Where is the vicar on holiday?".

No, Rashid, it wasn't Uzbekistan. But a good try! And no, Iqbal, it wasn't Iraq, although it was high on my list of places where I would have liked to go.

Things are really looking up there, apparently, with lovely beaches in the famous Green Zone and some of the restaurants have even got food!

So, a special prize to you for a good guess!

But the right answer, of course, is that I was very lucky to be invited yet again to that lovely Caribbean island where our old friend Sir Cliff Richard has a delightful little 18-bedroom villa, with its own pool, private beach, tennis court (very important!), dolphinarium and ocean-going yacht.

As you all know, Sir Clifford has been a good friend of the church ever since he first sang in our choir in the 1950s, and it would have been rude of me not to accept the generous invitation he sent me after I wrote to him asking whether I could come to stay with my entire family for a month!

Hey, and doesn't it say in the Good Book "It is

The Vicar entertains his friends with a rendition on the ukulele of the old favourite "We're All Going on a Free Summer Holiday"!

more blessed to receive than to give" (*Paul's Letter To The Freeloadians, 7.7*)?

So that's that little mystery cleared up!

But the main thing about holidays is not where you go or who you stay with, but how you feel when you come back!

And I have to say that I feel hugely refreshed by our time on that "island not in the Sun newspaper" (thank you for that very good joke, Mr Bremner!) and I can tell you that I am getting back to the vicarage with my batteries recharged.

And no, I haven't got a pacemaker, thank you Vijay, I am extremely healthy, and I only wish I could say the same for some of my former colleagues on the PCC. who seem to have chosen my holiday period as a suitable time to pass on! I was personally deeply saddened, as I am sure you all were, by the sad news about Mrs Mowlam.

As you will remember, Mo was a very much loved figure in the parish and in my early days here she seemed an ideal candidate to sort out the problems we'd been having with our mission in Northern Ireland (St Gerry's, formerly St Trimble's).

Of course, Mr Mandelson is right to point out that she made rather a hash of things (thanks to her growing fondness for Irish whiskey!) and left him to go in and clear up the mess!

I don't want to take anything away from Peter, who did a perfectly good job before he had to resign (again!), but in the end, if you want a job doing properly, you have to do it yourself – and so I did!

Anyway, that's all solved now and we can remember Mo as she was before her sad decline – a warm,

Local artist Mr de la Nougerede captures the scene during the Vicar's busy working holiday where he attends an important official ceremony to commemorate the fact that he can charge his travel expenses to the parish *(Is this right? Ed.)*

bubbly, fun-loving, young Sunday school teacher who only later turned into an embittered old harridan sitting on a park bench drinking meths and shouting four-letter abuse about the vicar!

What a sad end, and some might say she had it coming to her! Let us hope that the same fate doesn't await poor Mrs Short, after the tragically early departure of Mrs Mowlam and our disgraced former organist Mr Cook.

But enough of such sadness! I wanted to end on a bright note, and that's to congratulate all our school leavers on their wonderful exam results.

Mrs Kelly, the chair of governors at our Kwikfit Beacon Academy for Excellence (formerly the Shirley Williams Comprehensive) tells me that some of you got A levels who didn't even take them!

So, well done everyone, and I think we can award ourselves an 'A Star' for the tremendous strides education has made in the parish since 1997!

And let's face it, reading and writing aren't everything in the age of the internet and mobile phone!

So let's celebrate with a 24-hour drinking session at the Britannia Arms, now that it's sensibly allowed to open all day and all night!

Cheers!

Tony

Well Done!!!

A huge 'thank you' to my namesake, PC Blair, who, as everyone recognises, has done a terrific job in keeping us all safe in the summer months (except, of course, for poor Mr Menenez, the innocent Brazilian terrorist who was sadly shot down by PC Blair's colleagues acting in good faith). So, well done, Ian. Keep up the good work and we can all sleep safely in our beds at night (so long as we don't then go out and catch the tube in the morning!). T.B.

NOTICE TO LOCAL MEDIA

Editors of the St Albion's Echo and the producers at St Albion's Cottage Hospital Radio are hereby instructed that, for reasons of security, they must no longer reveal the address where the vicar lives – ie, the Vicarage. Your cooperation in this regard would be appreciated, otherwise you will face criminal prosecution under the Freedom of Agreeable Caribbean Villas Act 2005.

**Charles Clarke,
Head of St Albion's
Neighbourhood Watch**

ST ALBION PARISH NEWS

A Very Important Message From Rev. Dubya Of The Church Of Latter-Day Morons

Brothers and sisters in New Englandland Land – I thank you all for your prayerfulness and your condolleelzences at this time of despairitude.

But make no mistake – this is the work of the Lord, as is foretold in the Words of the Prophet, "Yea, there shall come a mighty wind and great waves and ye shall do damn all about it".

Thus saith the Lord and who am I to question the will of the Almighty?

No, siree! My job is to watch and pray. Pray and watch. Look at my watch and pray that everything turns out ok as time ticks away for poor old Dubya!

So my congratuity goes out to you all again in my hour of needfulnosity.

And my message to all you drowning black folks in Noo Orleans – Hang on in there, a piece of my old ma's cherry pie is coming your way, courtesy of Brother Rumsfeld's Heat-'n'-Eat CherryPieToGo Corporation, which is looking after all your wants in this hour of your death!

God be with you, for I am not.

Rev. Dubya

Hullo!

And there's only really been one thing happening in the past couple of weeks – no, not the hurricane, Dean, although of course that's very sad and we're all very sorry for our good friend the Rev. Dubya, who frankly cannot be blamed for what's happened, which was an Act of God, and, honestly, to blame the Rev. Dubya for it is like blaming Noah for the flood, when all he was trying to do was to save everyone!

Anyway, it's only too easy, isn't it, to blame the man in charge when something goes wrong – when usually it is not their fault at all, but that of lots of other people below them who aren't up to the job, such as Mr Byers... but I digress.

It's not the hurricane that's the important thing. I know from all your letters and emails and texts that what really concerns you on a day-to-day basis is the flood of loutish and anti-social behaviour that is engulfing the streets of our parish!

Everywhere we look we see young people behaving badly – stuffing their lager cans into people's garden hedges, spitting out their chewing gum onto our pavements, spraying graffiti on the walls of the bus shelter, and – I'm sorry to say it – drunkenness, drunkenness, drunkenness. The 'Three D's', as I call them!

Well, it really doesn't have to be like that!

And I've thought long and hard about how to tackle this problem. No, Vijay, I'm not going to resign. That's not funny or clever. In fact, it's an example of precisely the kind of rude, nasty, thoughtless behaviour that I am determined to stamp out, right across the parish.

And that's why I've come up with my Two-Point Plan, which I've called my 'Respect Plan'.

1. To alleviate the problem of drunkenness, the Britannia Arms should remain open for 24 hours a day, so that everyone will be free to continue drinking steadily and in a civilised manner, rather than having to indulge in binge-drinking sessions just because the pub is about to close. Makes sense, doesn't it?

2. I have asked my good friend Mrs Casey to become the St Albion's Respect 'czar', spearheading our new campaign to teach the kids how to behave properly.

And, hey, let's admit it. It's not just the kids who get drunk and swear and create a thorough nuisance of themselves.

It's Mrs Casey as well! And that's the whole point of why I have appointed her! You all remember the scene she created at the Harvest Supper, when she knocked back a whole bottle of Communion wine and started swearing at everyone.

Some of the older parishioners may have been shocked when she described the PCC as "a bunch of w***ers" and suggested that it was a good idea to be drunk all the time because it helps you to work better.

But I take a different view. The very fact that Mrs Casey is a foul-mouthed alcoholic makes her ideally qualified to head up our Anti-Social Behaviour Task Force, because she knows just where these kids are coming from! Ok?

Which brings me to my second point. As I'm sure you know, I have recently returned from our mission to China, where I have been preaching the word to our Chinese brethren.

Vicar on the spot! As seen by local artist Mr de la Nougerede

Cherie came along with me, and was delighted to be able to get some early Christmas shopping, when she bought several hundred bras and T-shirts for only the equivalent of 20p! It's hard to think that children of five can make such wonderful garments! There's a lesson there for our own five-year-olds who are getting drunk and falling around in the streets!

Anyway, much to my surprise, our hosts invited me to play a game of football.

Some reports in our local media have tried to suggest that I kept missing the goal. But let me say, it is they, the journalists, who have 'missed' the point! Of course I wasn't trying to kick the ball into the goal.

I was deliberately missing the goal, and for a very good reason. 'Respect' for my Chinese hosts, who are very sensitive about losing face. In fact you can even be locked up if you cause offence or upset them!

So can we please hear no more about our vicar 'missing the target', because that's one thing I never do!

Which brings me back to my first point, which is the theme of this newsletter. The three 'R's' – 'Respect', 'Respect' and 'Respect'.

Which is why, for this week's evening service, I have written a new chorus to remind us all of how important it is to show respect to each other.

Respect, respect, respect,
It's what we all expect,
Respect, respect, respect,
It's what we mustn't neglect!

Words and music T. Blair 2005 (Taken from '100 Hymns For Binge-Drinkers', which can be downloaded onto your iPod from the vicarage website www.welovetony.org)

Yours 'respectfully',